Women Composers of American Parlor Music for Fingerstyle Guitar

Sandy Shalk

Online Audio

To access the online audio recording go to:
WWW.MELBAY.COM/31185MEB

I0808777

MEL BAY®

WWW.MELBAY.COM

Contents

Preface

The women composers represented in this collection of solo guitar arrangements wrote and published music during the North American parlor music era—with the heyday being the Victorian Age. Before the advent of the phonograph and radio, musical compositions were typically disseminated as sheet music (often for voice and piano) and sold by publishing houses. The music included hymns, minstrel music, patriotic songs, topical songs, folk, ragtime and the blues.

Music composing and publishing was a male-dominated industry. Women were more likely to be viewed as performers and educators rather than composers, and as such were seldom encouraged to publish. By the mid-19th century, women began to emerge as composers of popular music and had success publishing. Carrie Jacobs-Bond was one of the most successful composers of popular songs in the early 20th century, selling millions of copies of music and eventually running her own publishing house.

This is a collection of songs by women who wrote the music to popular songs from the 1840s to the 1920s in North America, and, in some instances, also wrote the lyrics to their compositions. Women composers of popular song are sometimes referred to as songwriters to distinguish them from composers of classical music such as the well-known American composer Amy Beach.

This collection is a representative example of the types of music being written by women composers during that time period in North America. There is so much remarkable music by women composers to be rediscovered. These solo guitar arrangements are meant for advanced beginners and intermediate players.

I would like to express my appreciation to guitarist El McMeen for his encouragement and editorial support. El has an extensive catalog of wonderful recordings and DVDs of solo guitar as well as books of arrangements, humor, and religious materials. His solo guitar recordings are joyous.

Enjoy the Journey,

Sandy Shalk

The Songs and the Composers

The Blue Juniata

Composer Marion Dix Sullivan (1802-1860) is considered to be the first woman to write a "hit" song with the popular success of *Blue Juniata* (published 1844). The lyrics are by J. W. Sullivan. It's a catchy, jaunty melody with a strong alternating bass. In *Blue Juniata*, a Native American maiden sings the praises of her warrior: "Bold is my warrior good. The love of Alfarata." It has been recorded many times, notably by Roy Rogers and Riders in the Sky.

Albert (or Say Not Adieu)

Clara Maria Brinkerhoff (born 1828) was an accomplished vocalist, educator, and composer, in addition to being a romance novelist—writing under the pseudonym Henri Gorden. Brinkerhoff wrote both the lyrics and the melody for *Albert (or Say Not Adieu)* which was published in 1864. In the song, the singer laments missing a loved one who is a long way from home. This arrangement changes key midway from G to C.

Star of the Sea

Amanda Kennedy wrote the music to *Star of the Sea* (published 1883) at the age of 16. It was a highly successful effort selling over two million copies. She later published the same tune as *Star of the East* with lyrics by George Cooper.

Open My Eyes, That I May See

Open My Eyes, That I May See is the hymn in this collection. Clara H. Scott (1841-1897) published *Open My Eyes* in 1895. Scott was a music teacher and composer primarily of hymns, many of which are still sung today. Born in Elk Grove Illinois, Scott graduated from the Chicago Musical Institute and began a teaching career. After marriage, she settled in Austin, Texas. She is the first woman to have published a book of anthems: *The Royal Anthem Book*. She tragically died in a horse carriage accident in 1897.

Sweet Rosie O'Grady

Maude Nugent had an extensive career as a vaudeville singer until she slowed down in her late twenties to raise a family. She continued to write songs, however. She composed the music and wrote the lyrics for *Sweet Rosie O'Grady* (published 1896) —undeniably her most popular piece. After being initially rejected, the song was published by Tin Pan Alley publisher Joseph W. Ster. The sheet music alone sold over a million copies. The verse is in 4/4 time and the chorus is a 3/4 waltz. It's a lovely tune that harkens back to the Emerald Isle.

The Fair March

Grace M. Bolen was 14 when she wrote *The Fair March*. It was published by Carl Hoffman in 1898. It is believed that her lessons with a piano teacher in the same building as the publishing company led to the connection. Her most famous tune was to come in 1901 with the publication of *Smokey Topaz*. She curtailed her publishing efforts after she married.

I Love You Truly

Of all the women composers in this collection, Carrie Jacobs-Bond (1862-1946) was clearly the most successful. Born in Janesville, Wisconsin, she came from a musical family, studied piano as a youth and began composing. After the death of her second husband, she lived on limited means. Bond eventually moved to Chicago to be closer to publishers. *I Love You Truly* was published in 1901. Bond eventually started her own successful publishing company with her son. *I Love You Truly* has been recorded many times and has sold multi-million copies of sheet music.

The Iroquois on Fire

Zella Evans wrote the words and music to *The Iroquois Fire*, published in 1904 by T. J. Kucher. It's a topical parlor song about a tragic event at the Iroquois Playhouse in Chicago in December of 1903. At a matinee performance of the musical Mr. Bluebird, a spark ignited a curtain, starting a deadly fire. The size the crowd and limited exits (some of which were faux exits) resulted in a horrific loss of life. The tragedy of the event is captured in the lyrics.

The End of a Perfect Day

Over 8 million copies of sheet music (pub. 1910) were sold for *The End of a Perfect Day* by Carrie Jacobs-Bond. The lyrics are by J. P. McEvoy. It became her most requested tune, particularly when she entertained U. S. troops in Europe during WWI. Bing Crosby, Jeanette MacDonald and Paul Robeson (among many others) recorded *The End of a Perfect Day*.

My Rose of Argentine

By 1915, the tango was a popular dance craze in New York and Paris, having originated in Argentina. Norma Gray set out to capture the flavor of this cultural phenomenon and wrote both the tune and lyrics to *My Rose of Argentine*. It was published in 1915 by the Penn Music Company.

Your Country Needs You

Your Country Needs You is a patriotic song written by Emily Wood Bower during WWI in 1917. Edith Wait-Colson wrote the lyrics. It was published by the Kennedy Music Corporation.

Down Hearted Blues

Down Hearted Blues was a popular success for African American composer Lovie Austin. Over 780,000 records were sold of *Down Hearted Blues* (published 1922) as recorded by Bessie Smith. The lyrics were written by the noted blues singer Alberta Hunter. Based in Chicago, Lovie Austin was a highly regarded bandleader, composer, and singer. She is considered to be one of the finest blues pianists of the period.

The Blue Juniata

Marion Dix Sullivan
Arr. Sandy Shalk

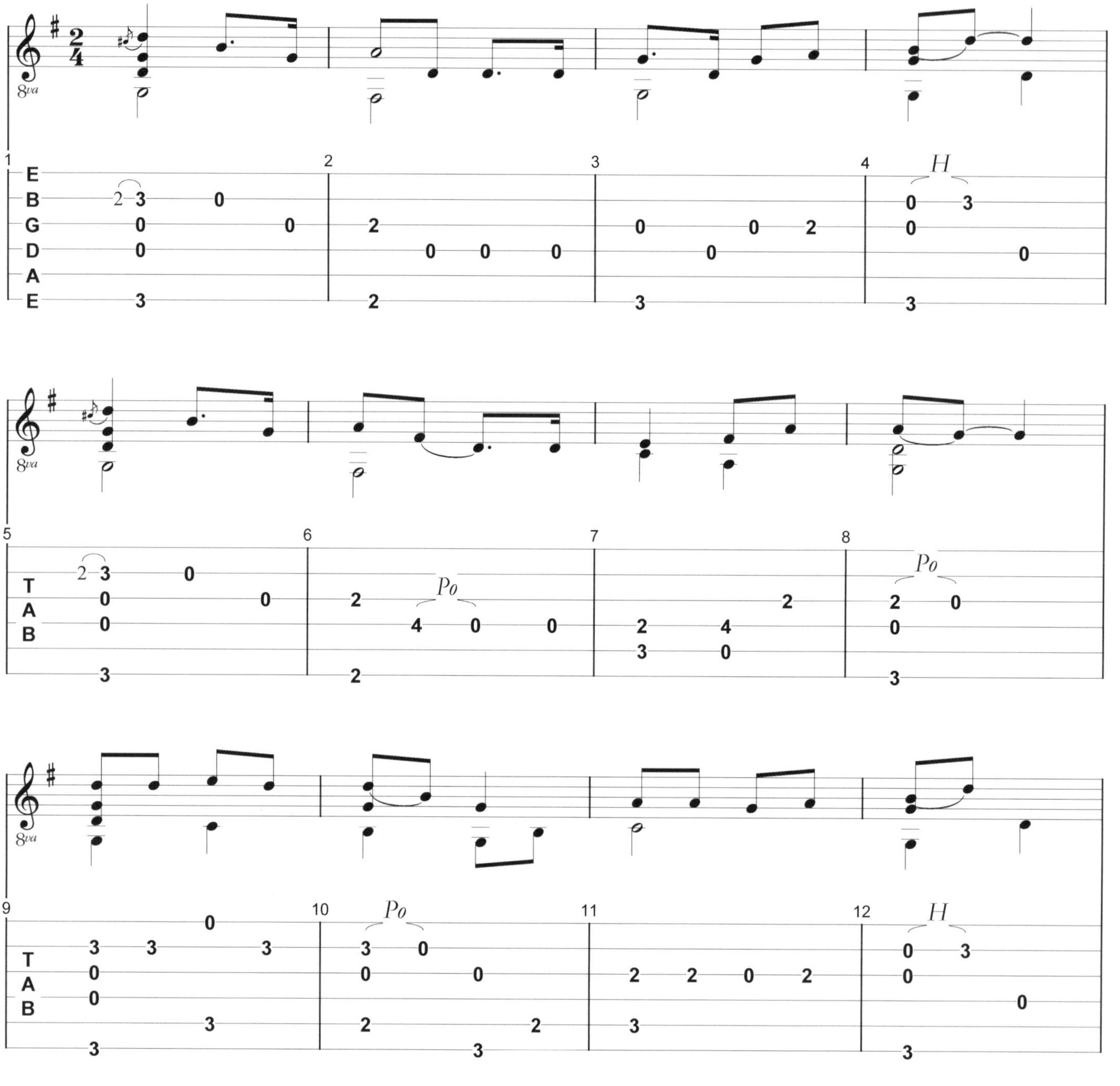

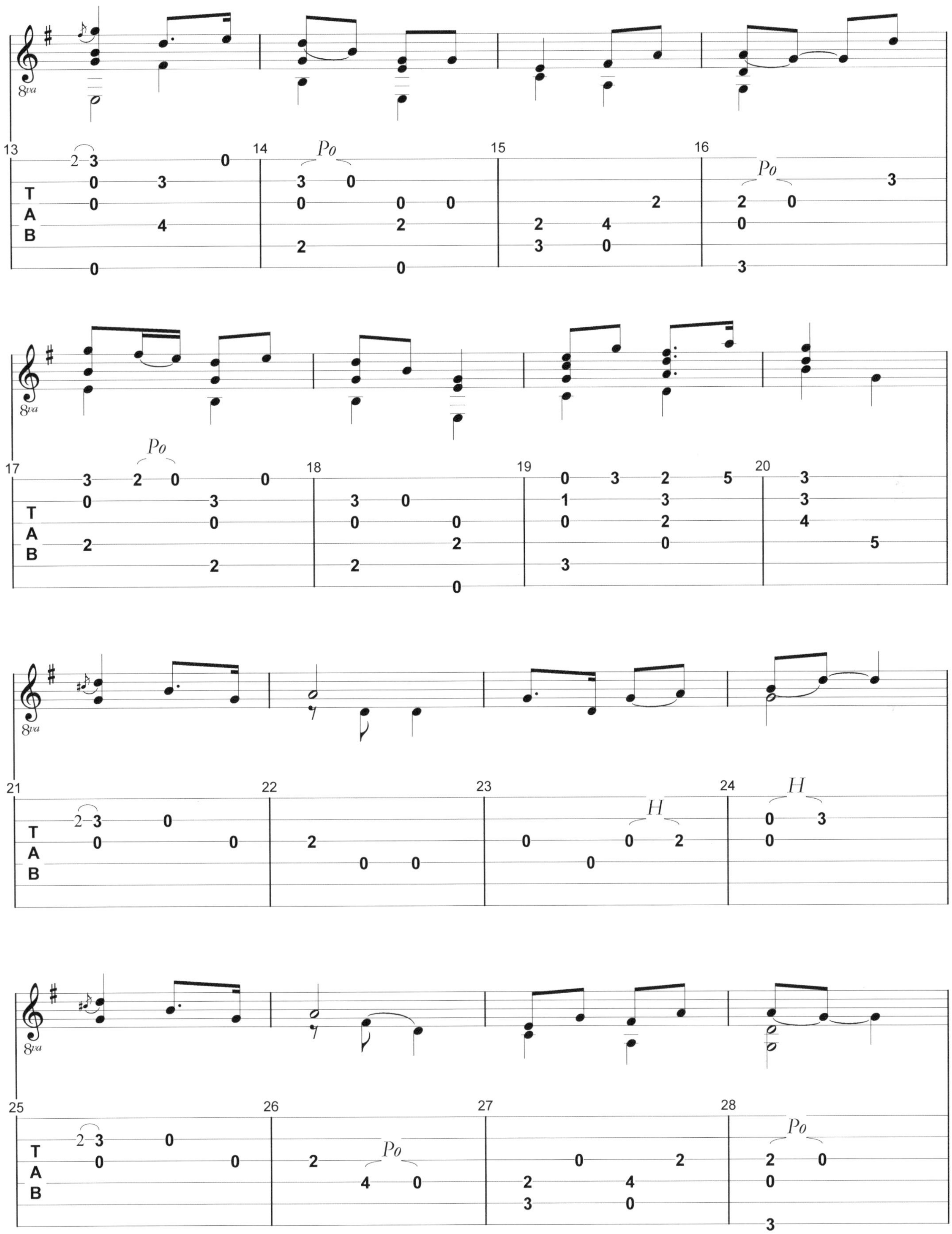
8va
13
14
15
16
17
18
19
20
21
22
23
24
25
26
27
28
Po
H
T
A
B

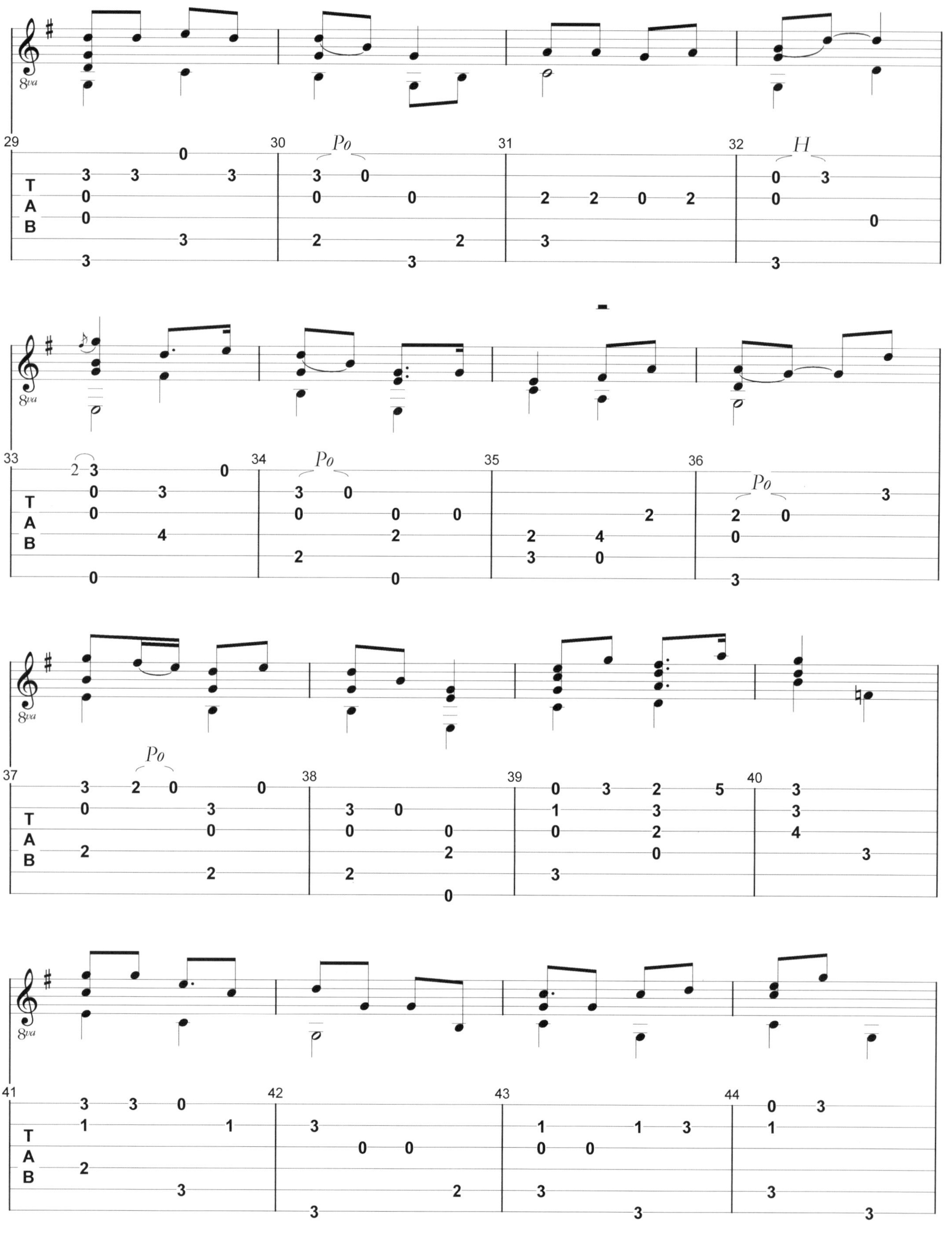
8va
Po
H
TAB

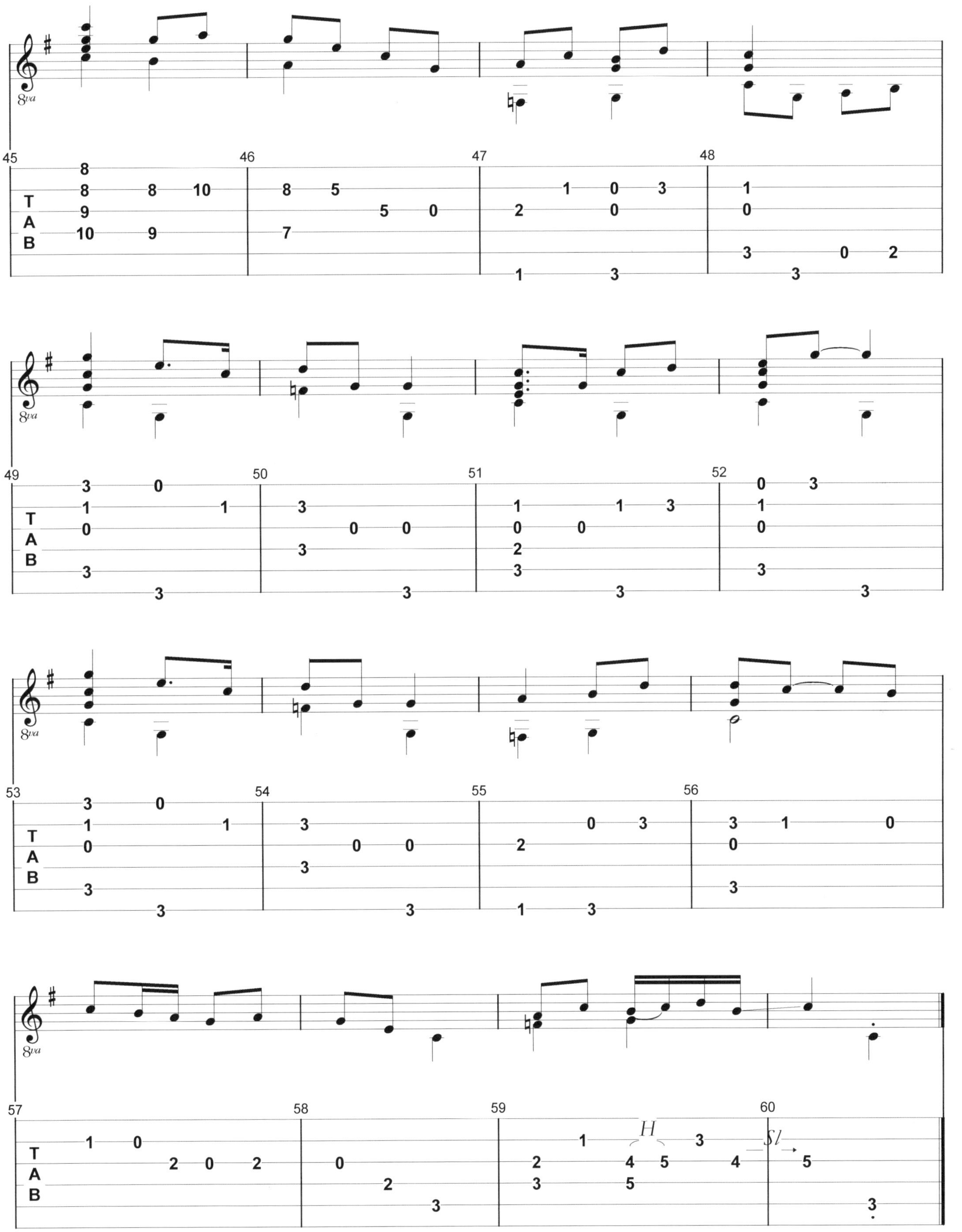
8va
TAB
H
Sl

Albert (or Say Not Adieu)

Clara M. Brinkerhoff
Arr. Sandy Shalk

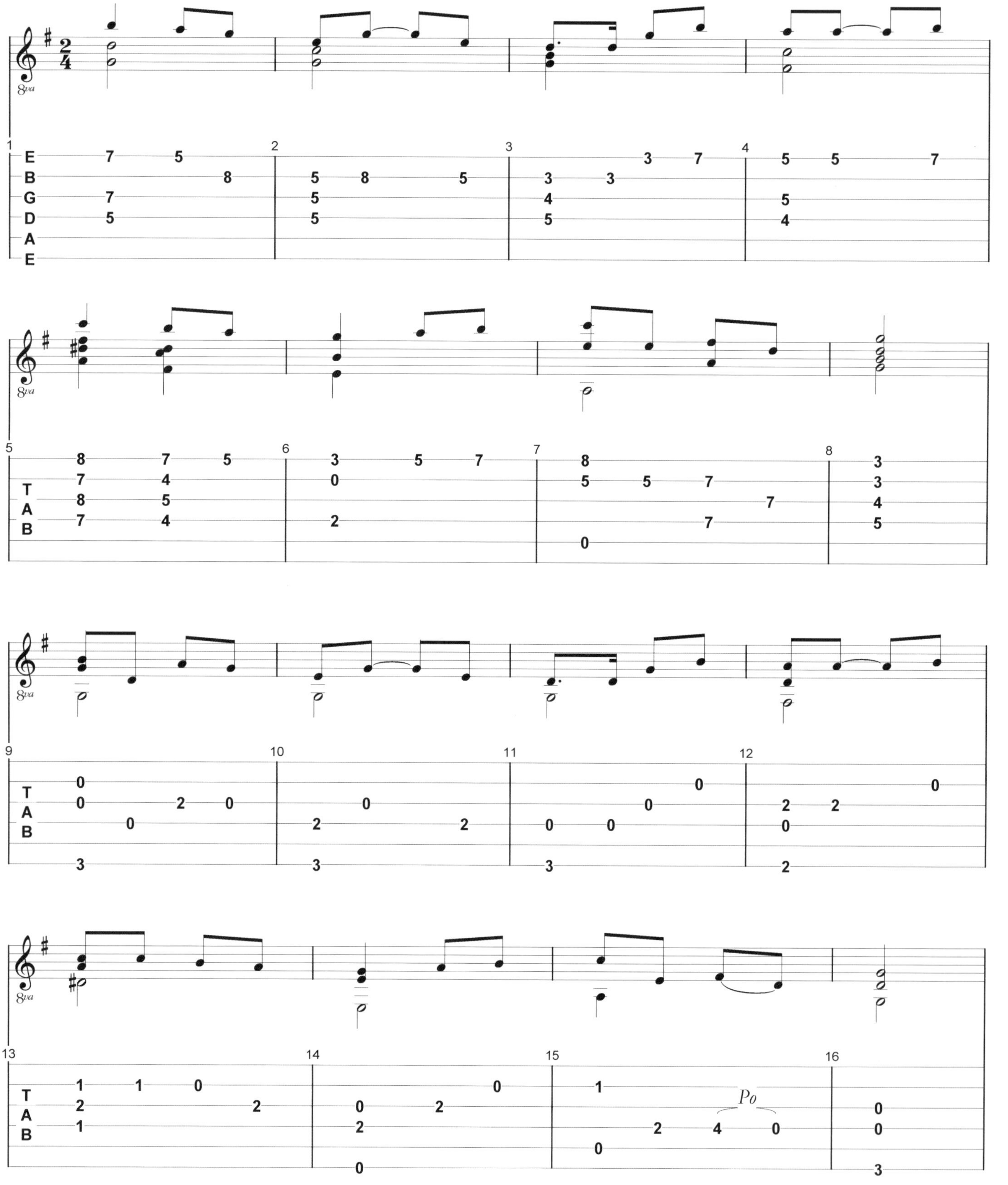

Albert (or Say Not Adieu)

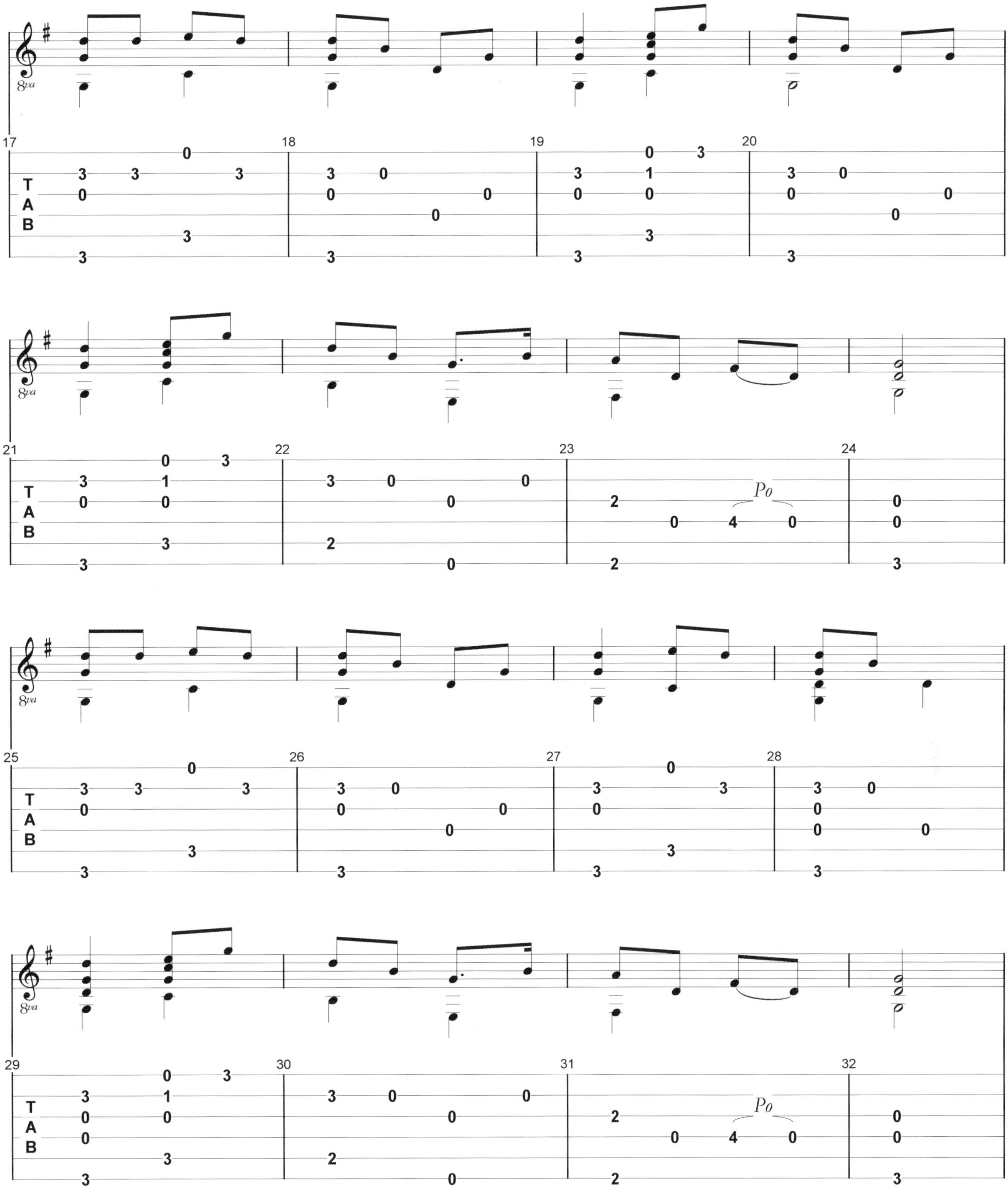

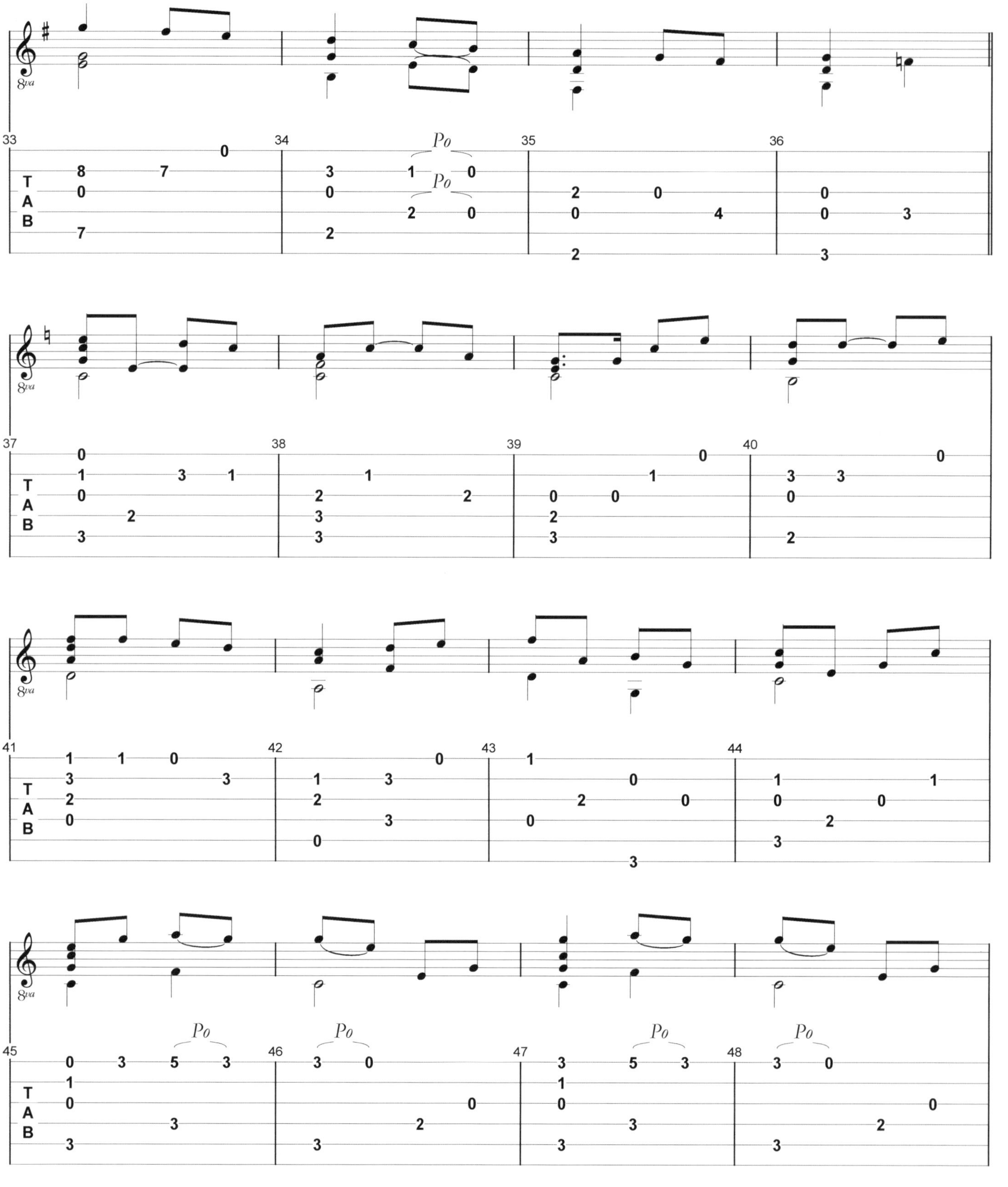
8va
T
A
B
Po

Albert (or Say Not Adieu)

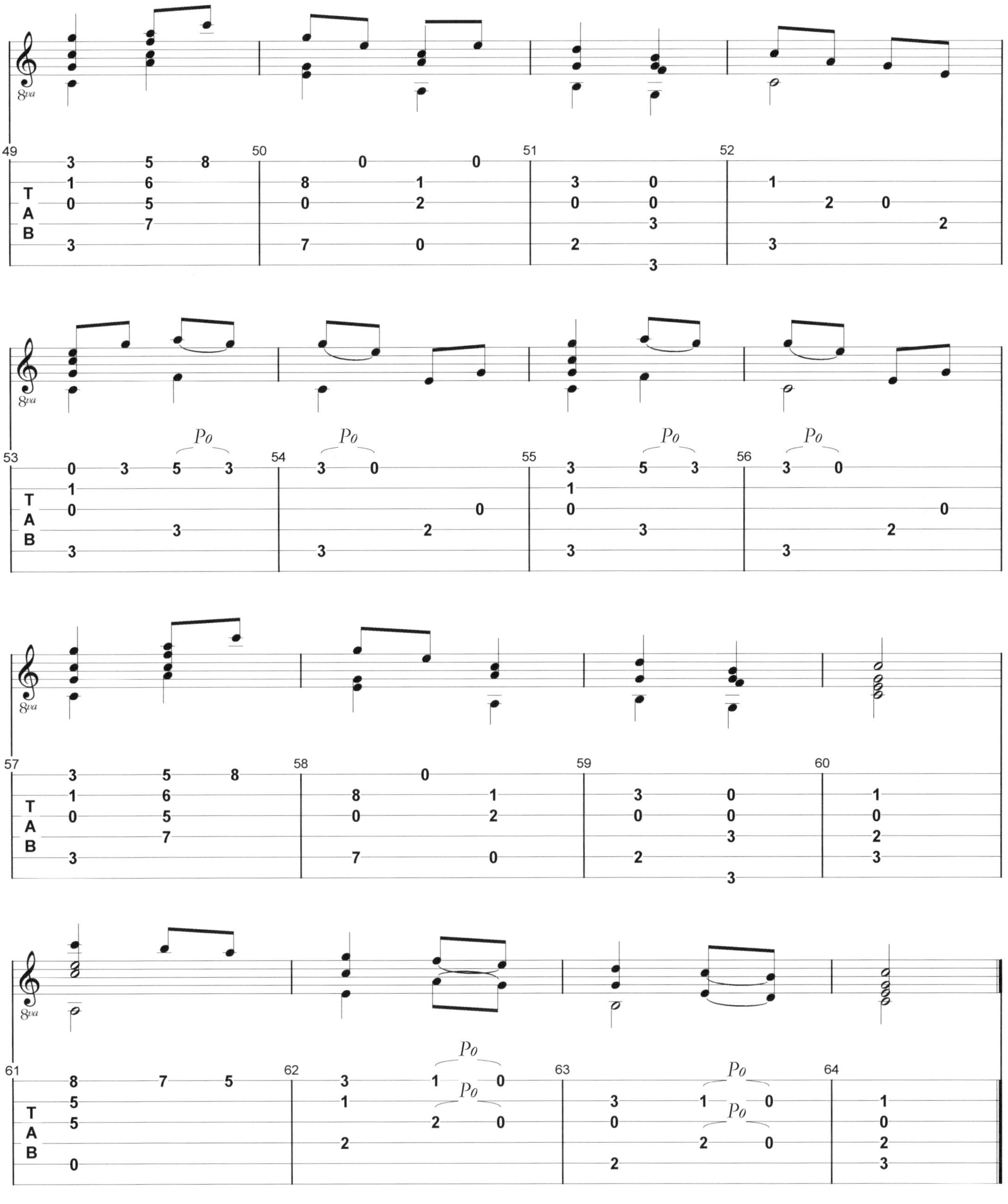

Star of the Sea

Amanda Kennedy
Arr. Sandy Shalk

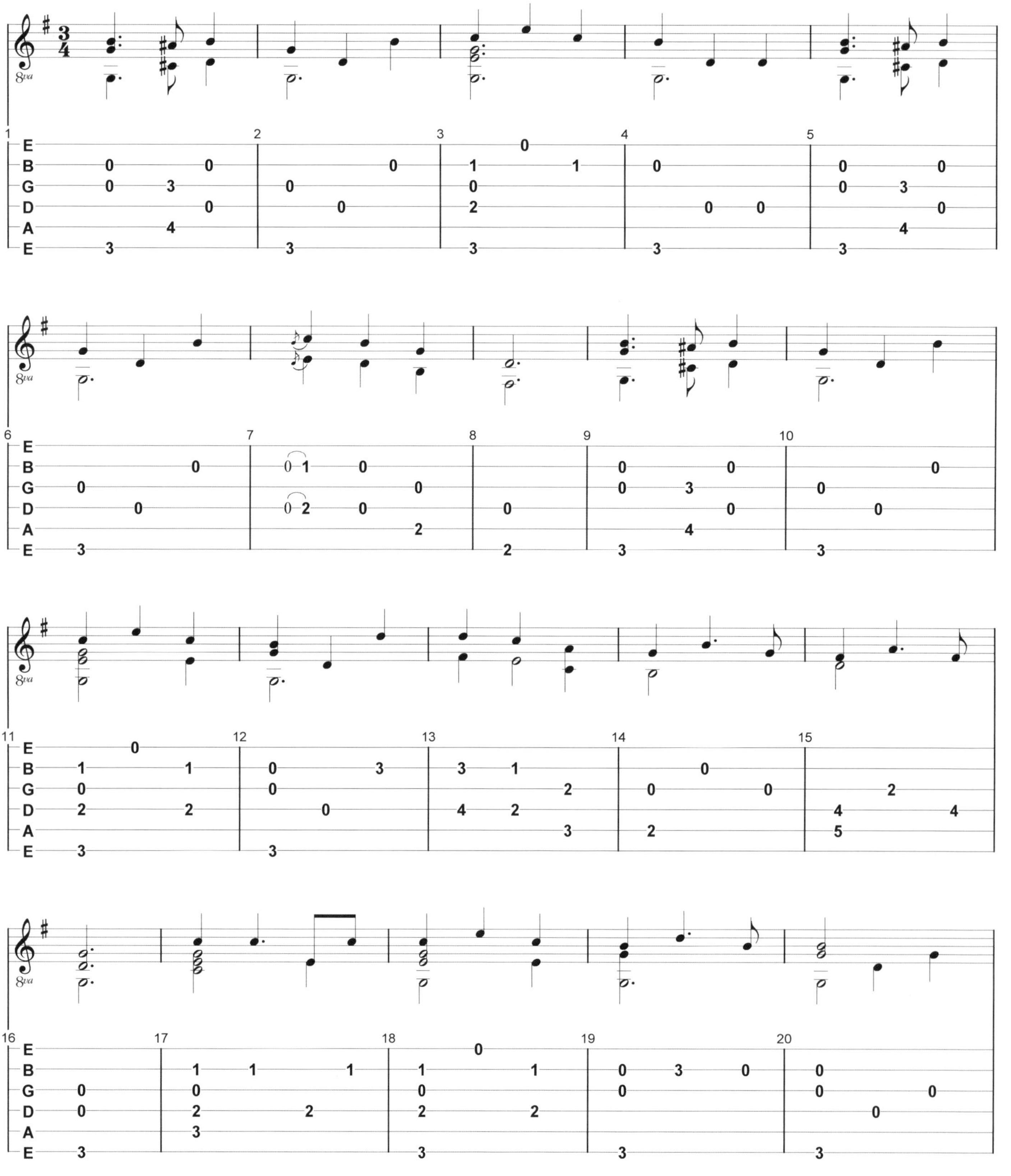

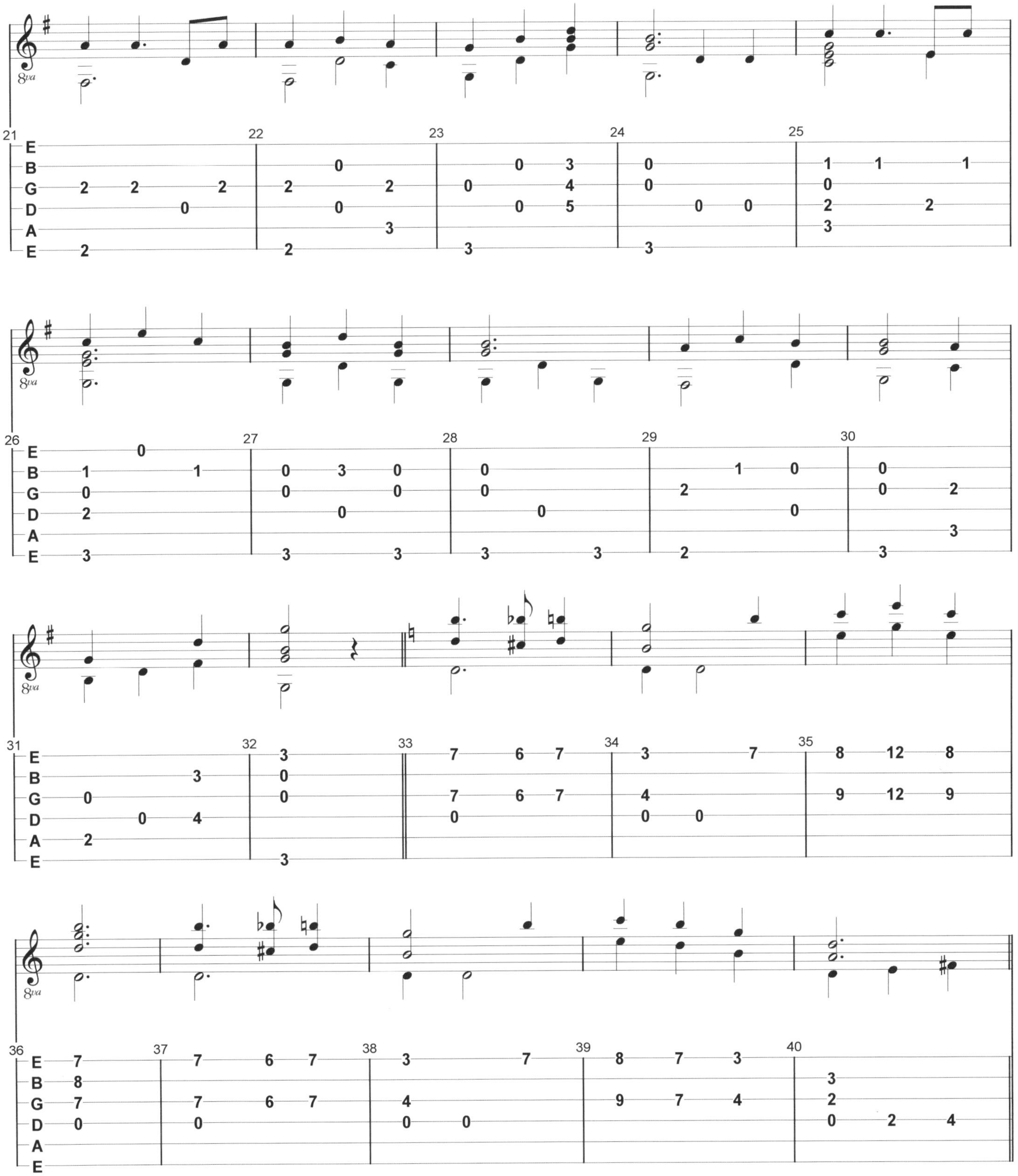

Star of the Sea

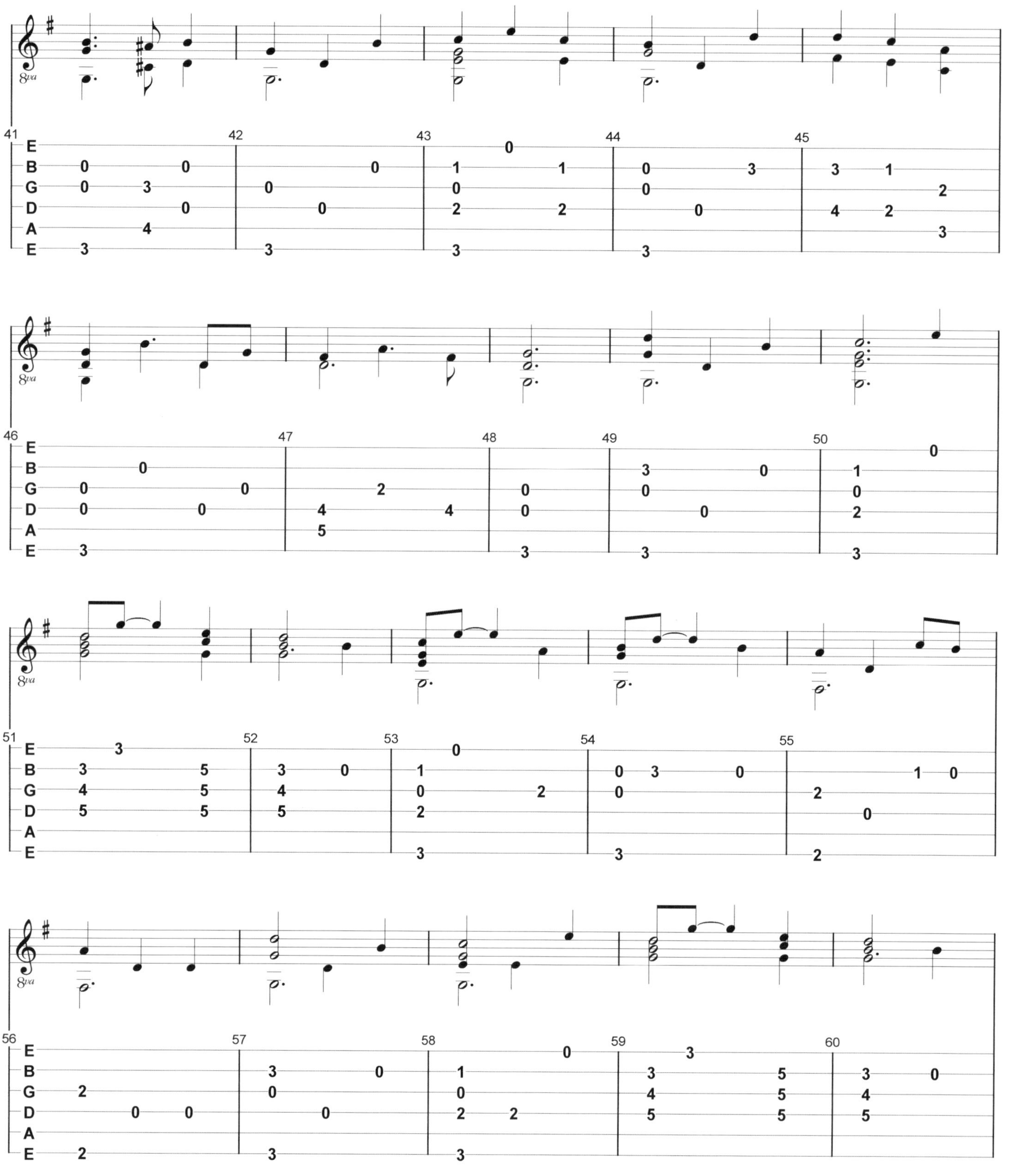

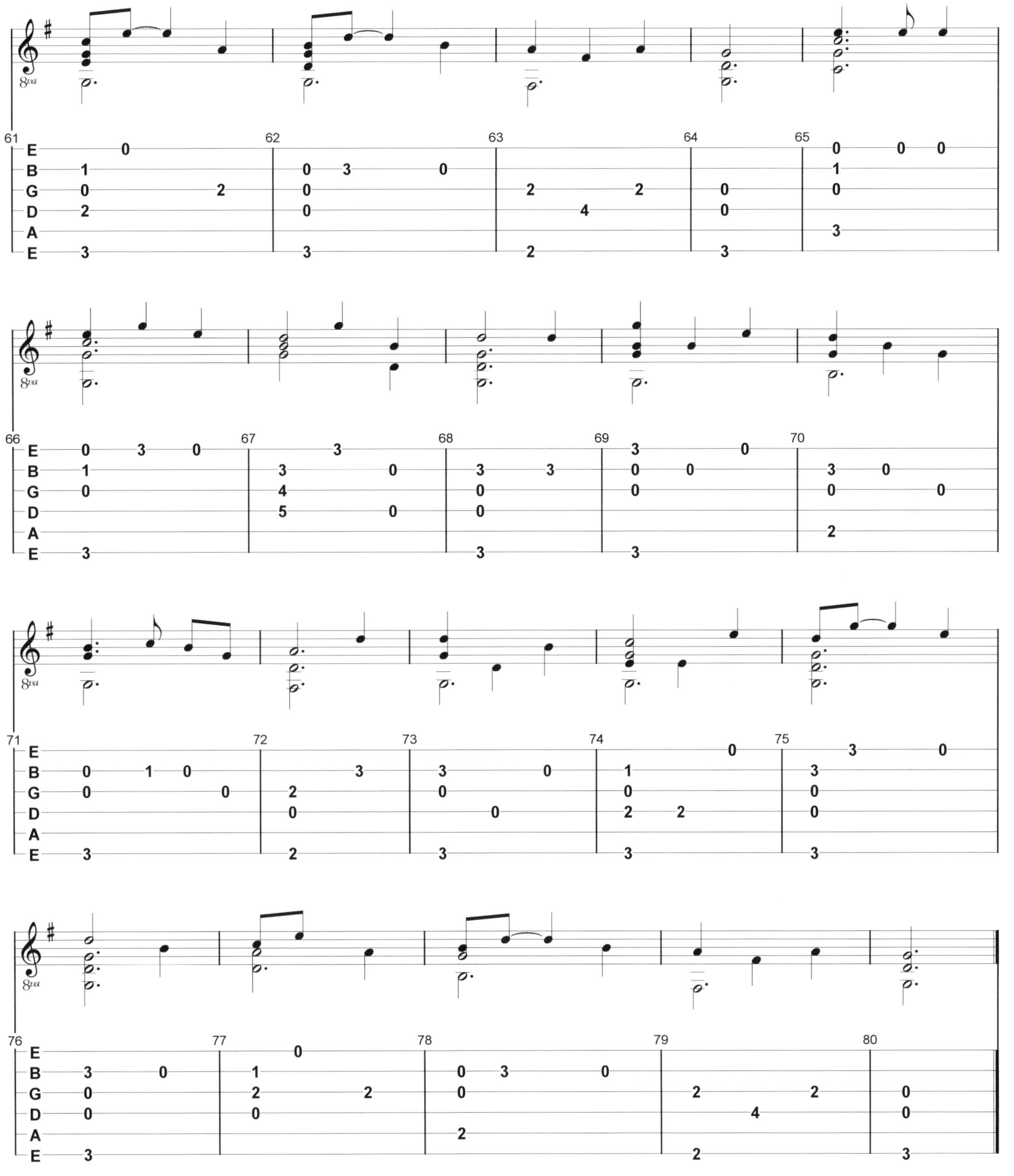

Open My Eyes, That I May See

Clara H. Scott
arr. Sandy Shalk

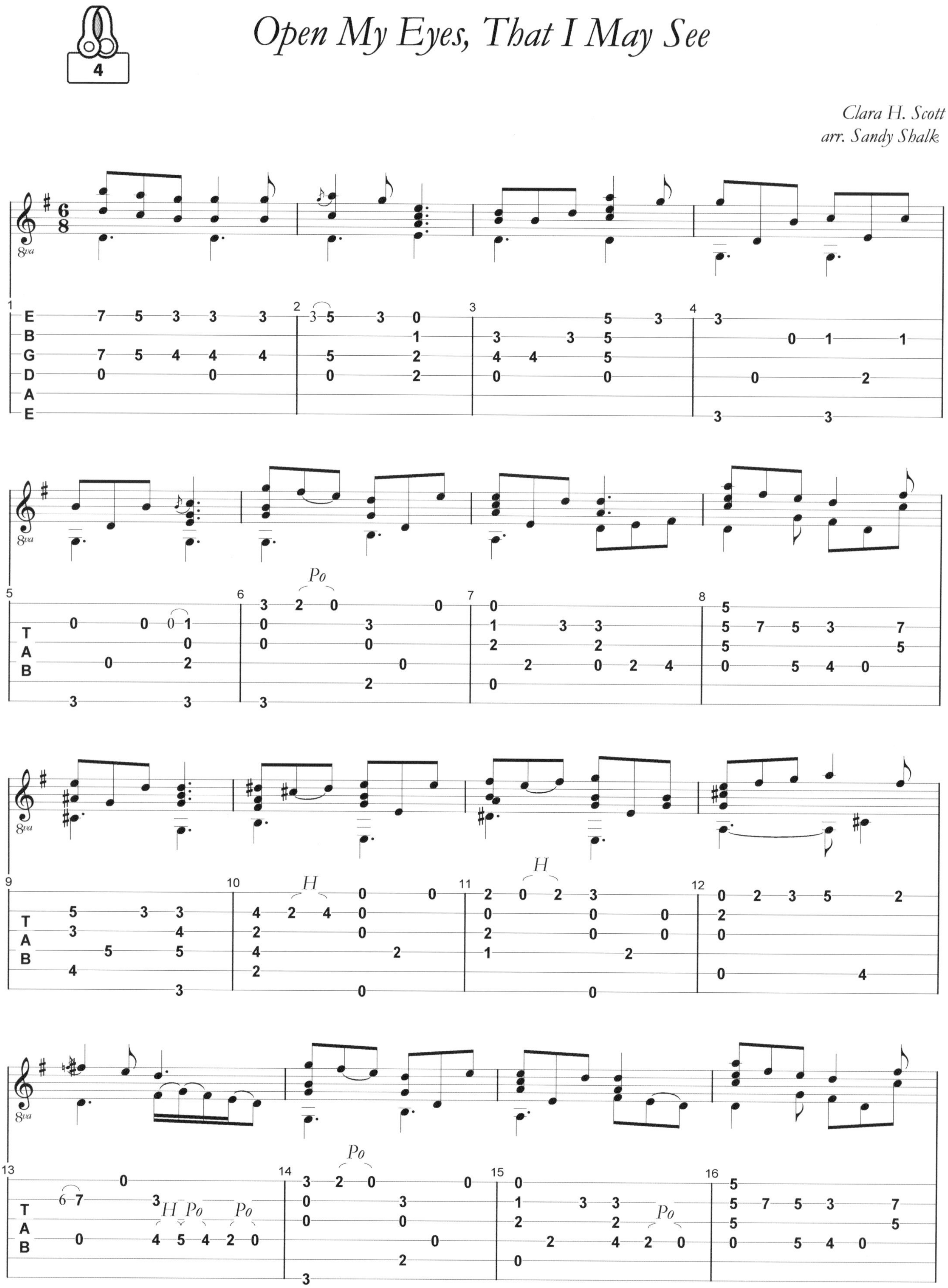

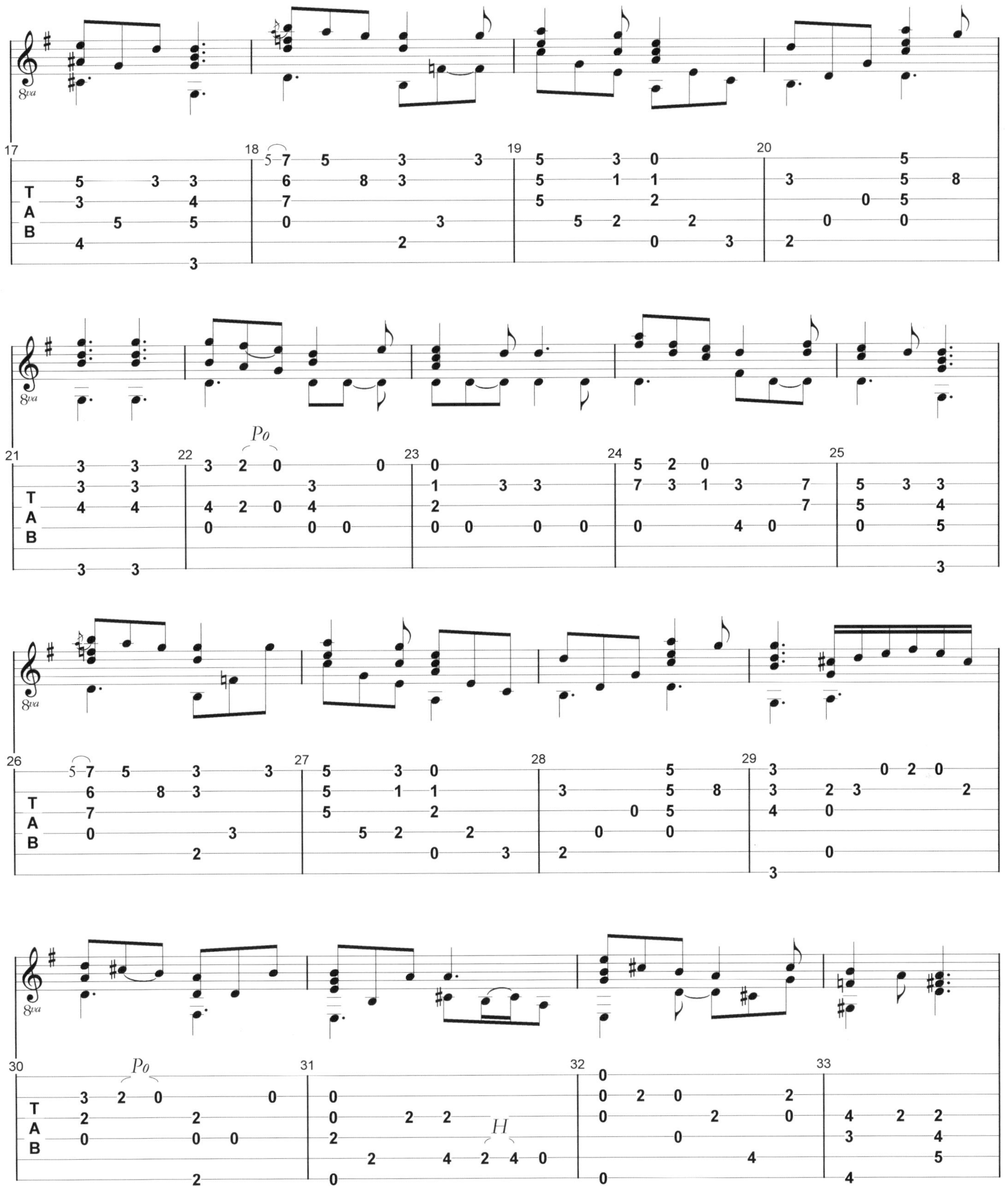
8va
Po
H

Open My Eyes, That I May See

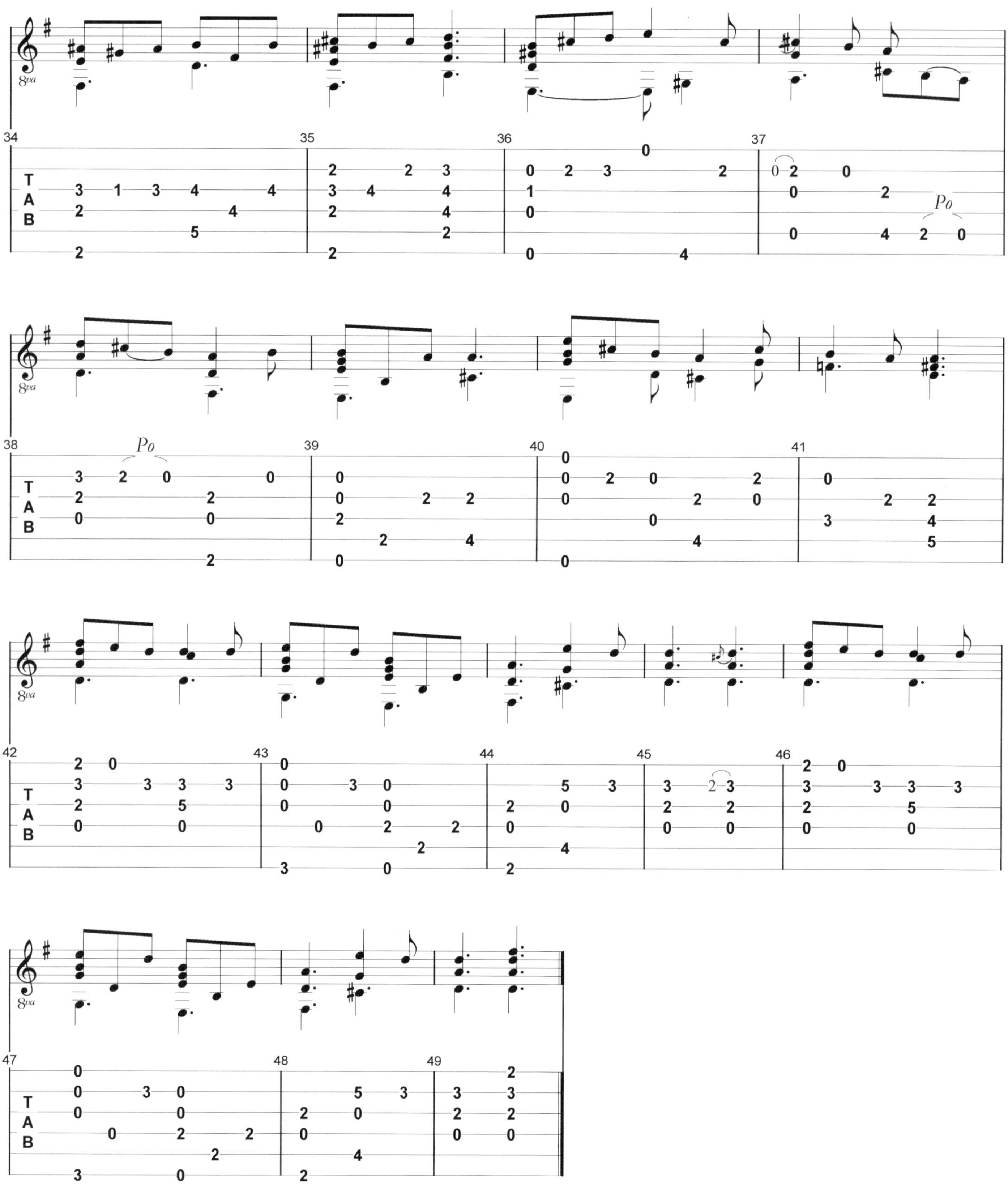

Now wouldn't you Like to know.

Song and Chorus.

Words & Music by

Mrs. Clara H. Scott.

CINCINNATI.
JOHN CHURCH & Co. 66 W. FOURTH St.

CHICAGO.
Root & Sons Music Co.

3

Sweet Rosie O'Grady

5

Maude Nugent
Arr. Sandy Shalk

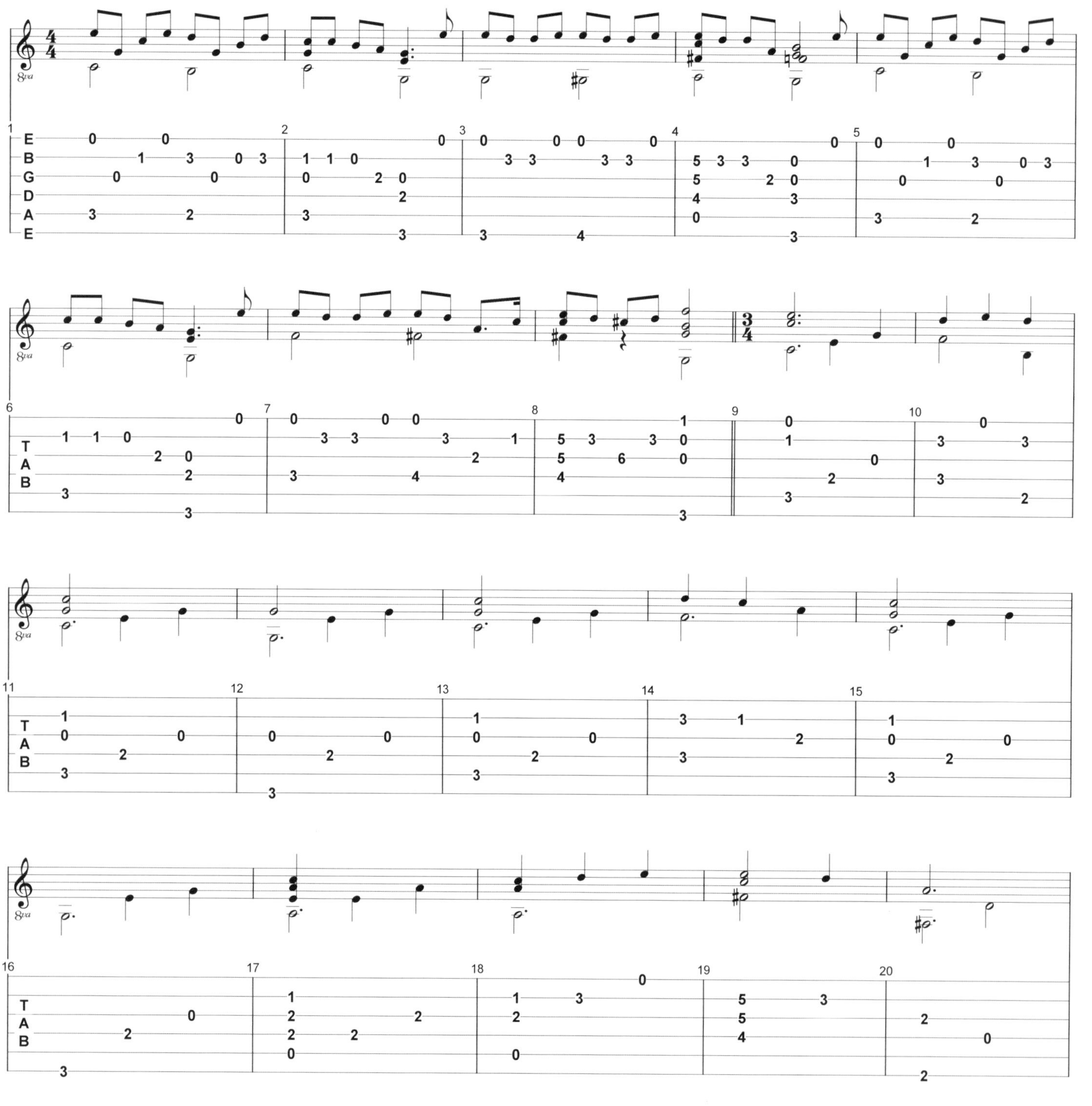

Sweet Rosie O'Grady

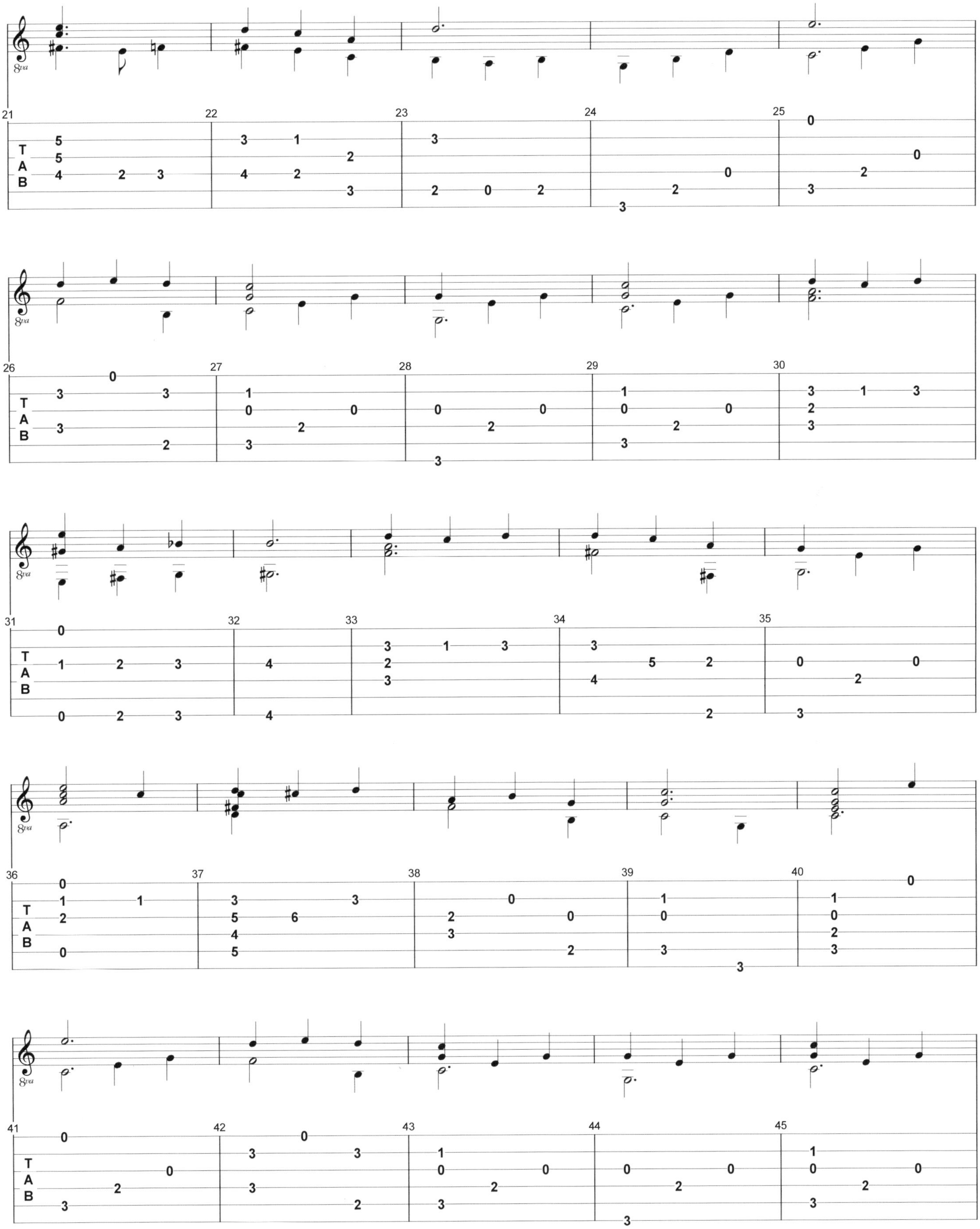

Sweet Rosie O'Grady

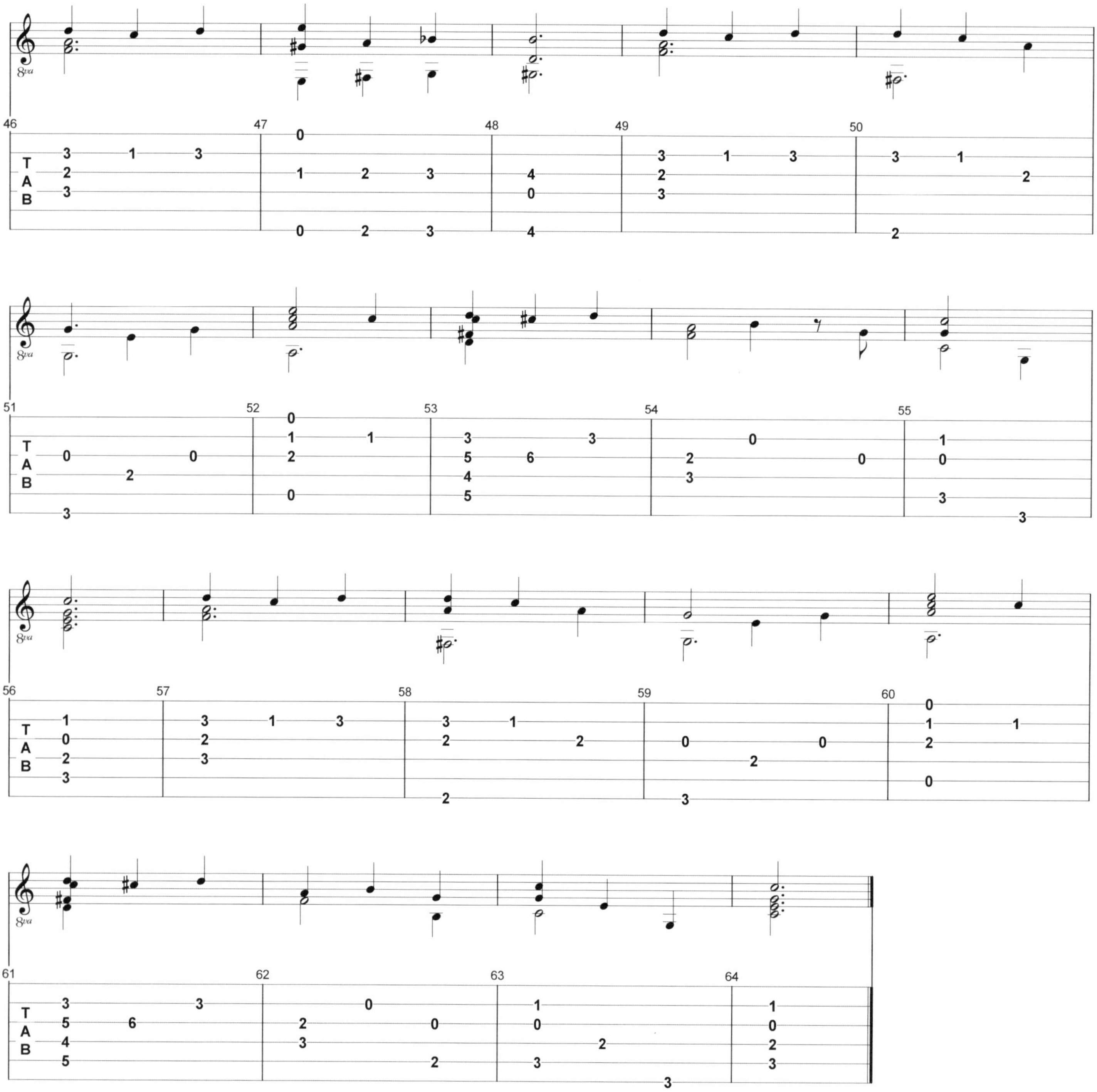

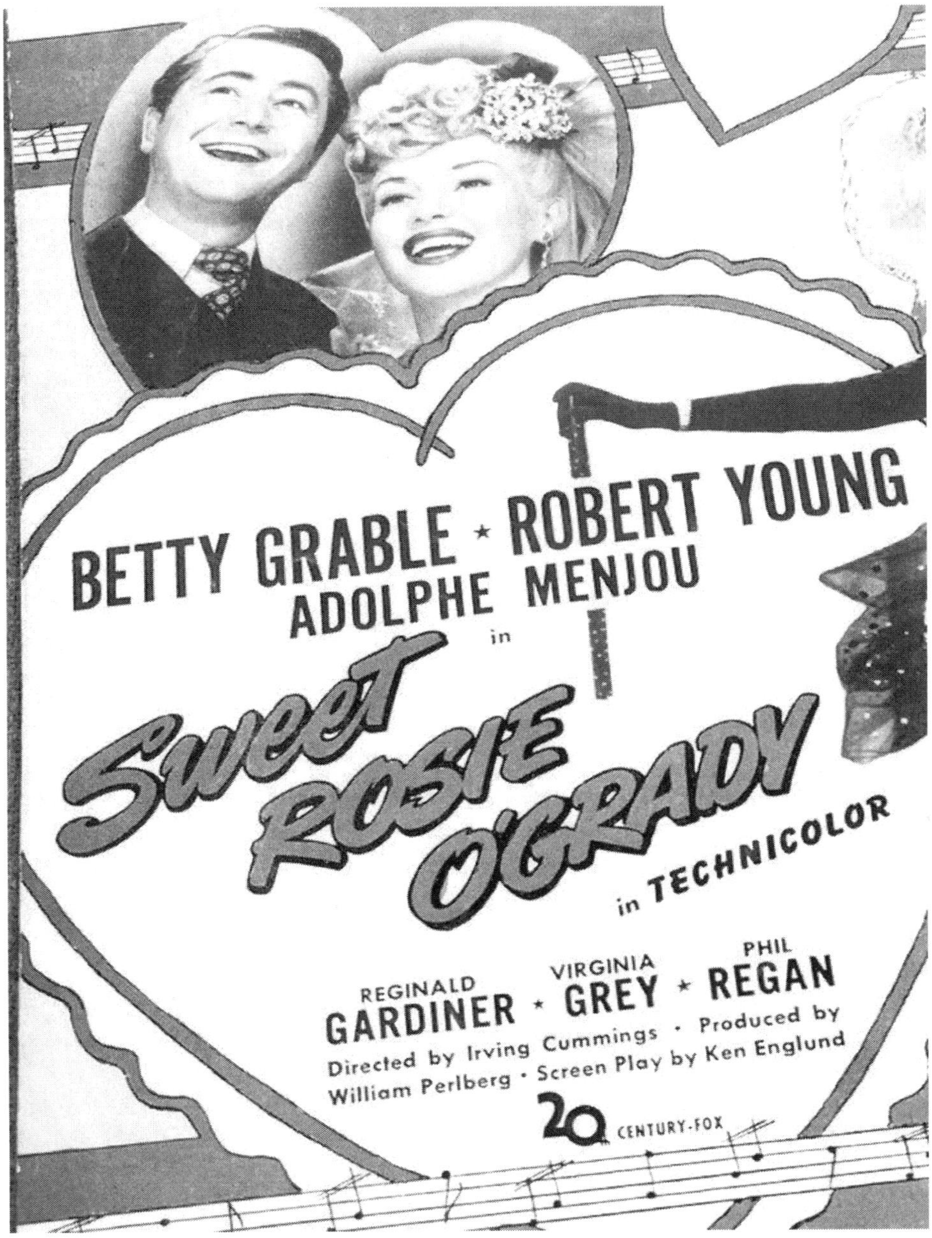
BETTY GRABLE ★ ROBERT YOUNG
ADOLPHE MENJOU
in
Sweet Rosie O'Grady
in TECHNICOLOR
REGINALD GARDINER ★ VIRGINIA GREY ★ PHIL REGAN
Directed by Irving Cummings · Produced by William Perlberg · Screen Play by Ken Englund
20 CENTURY-FOX

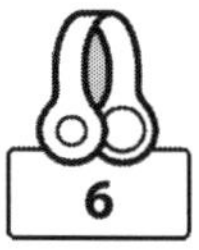

The Fair March

Grace Marie Bolen
Arr. Sandy Shalk

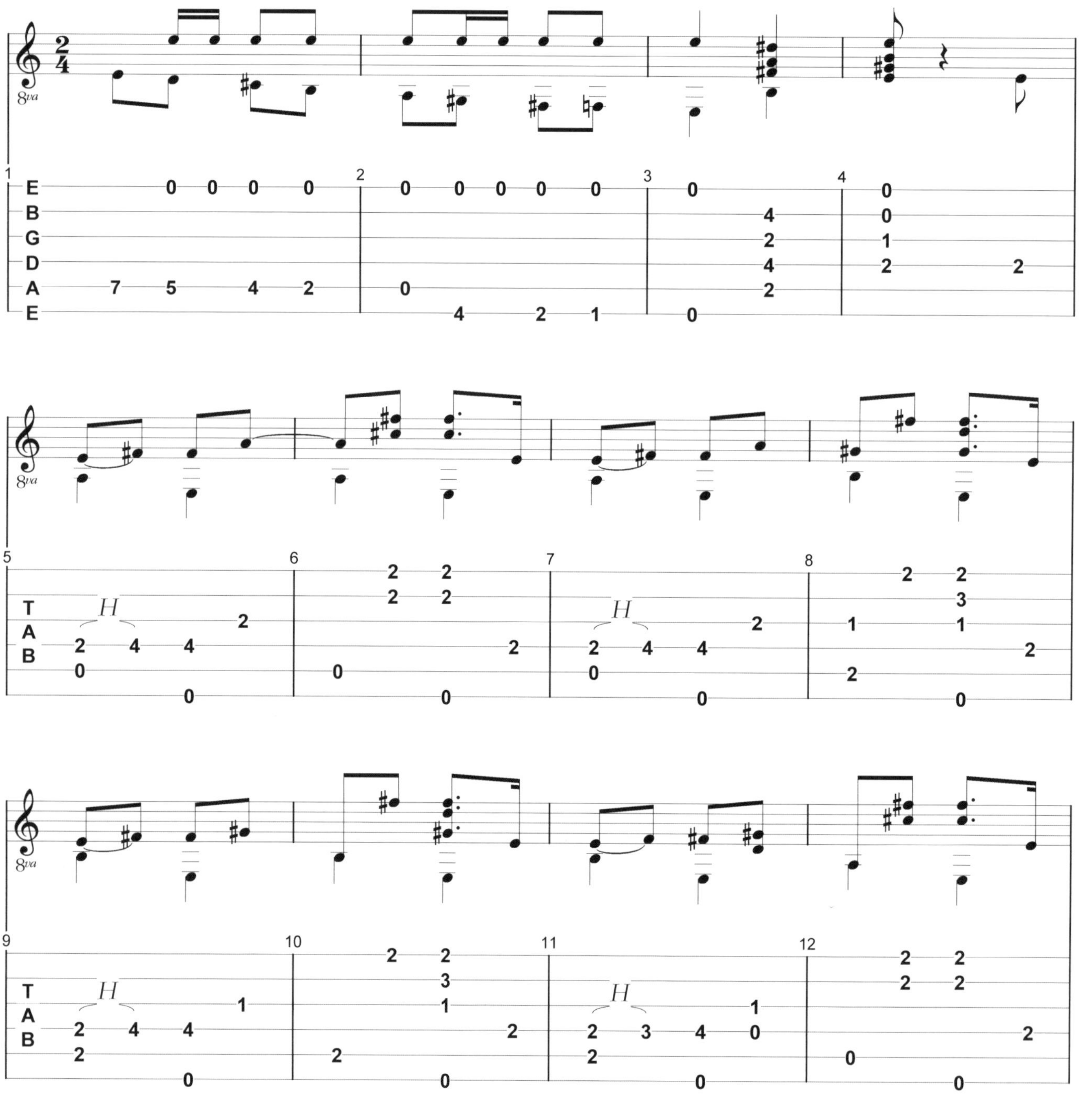

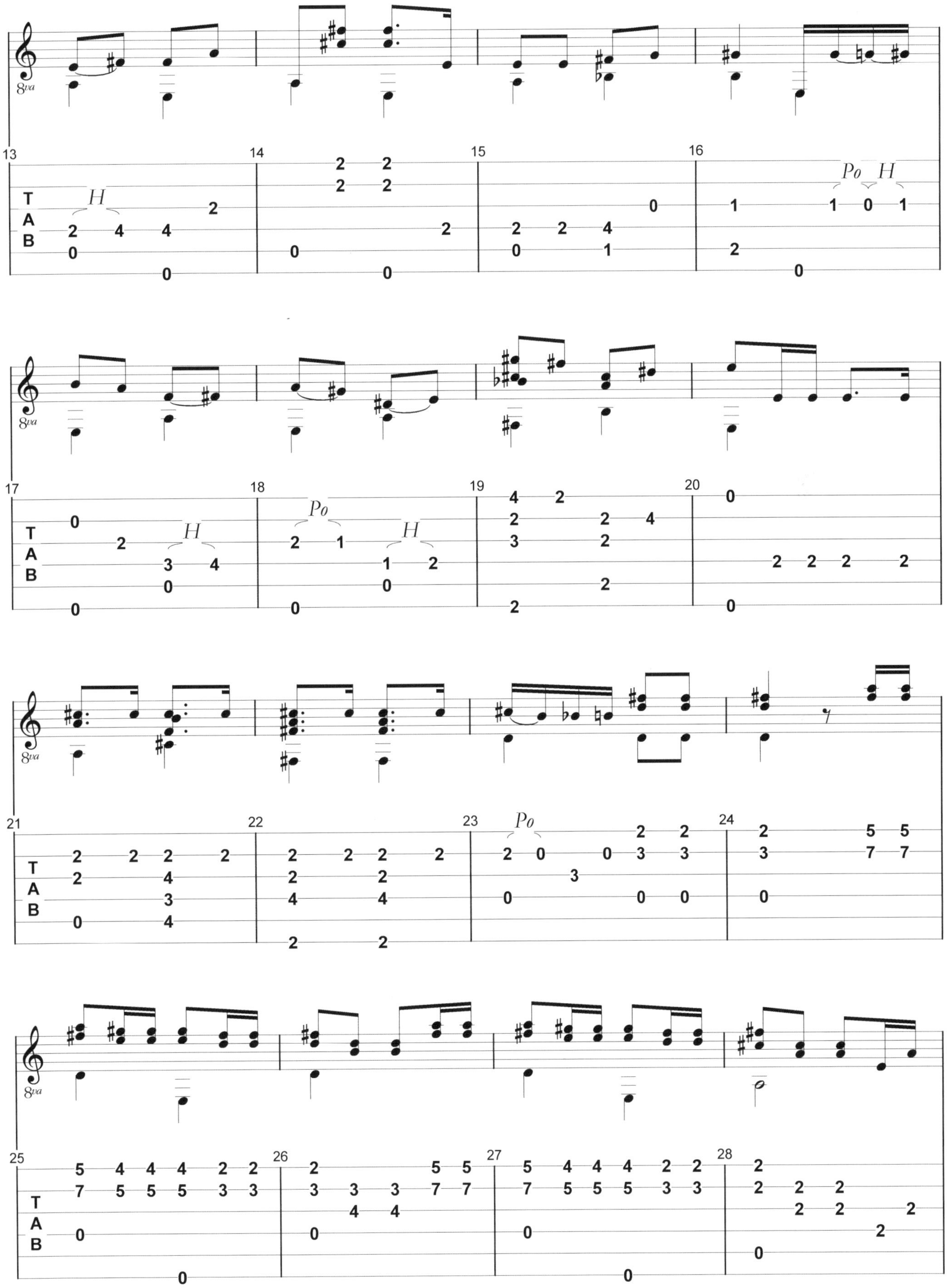
8va
T
A
B
13
14
15
16
17
18
19
20
21
22
23
24
25
26
27
28
H
Po

The Fair March

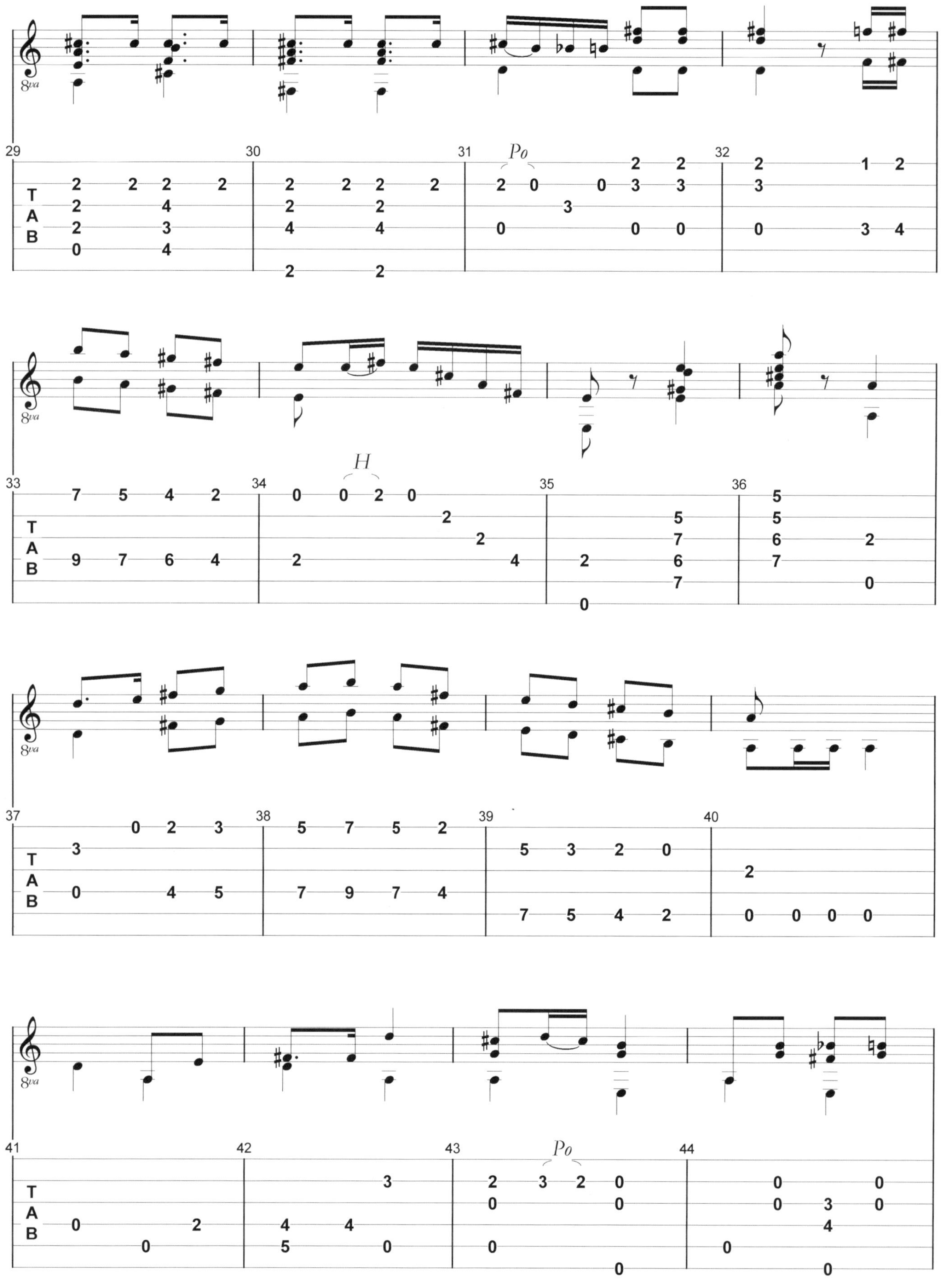

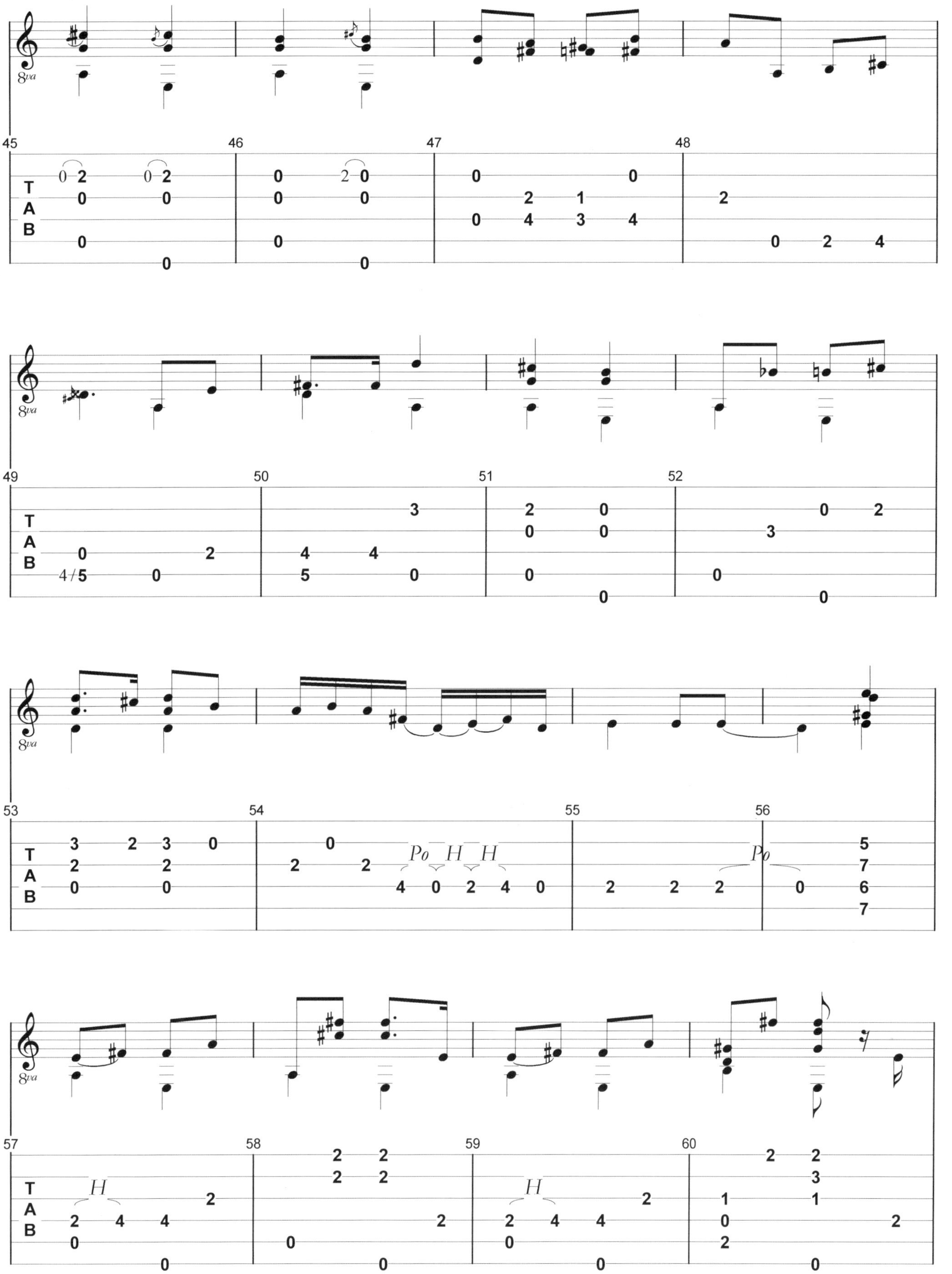
8va
T
A
B
Po
H

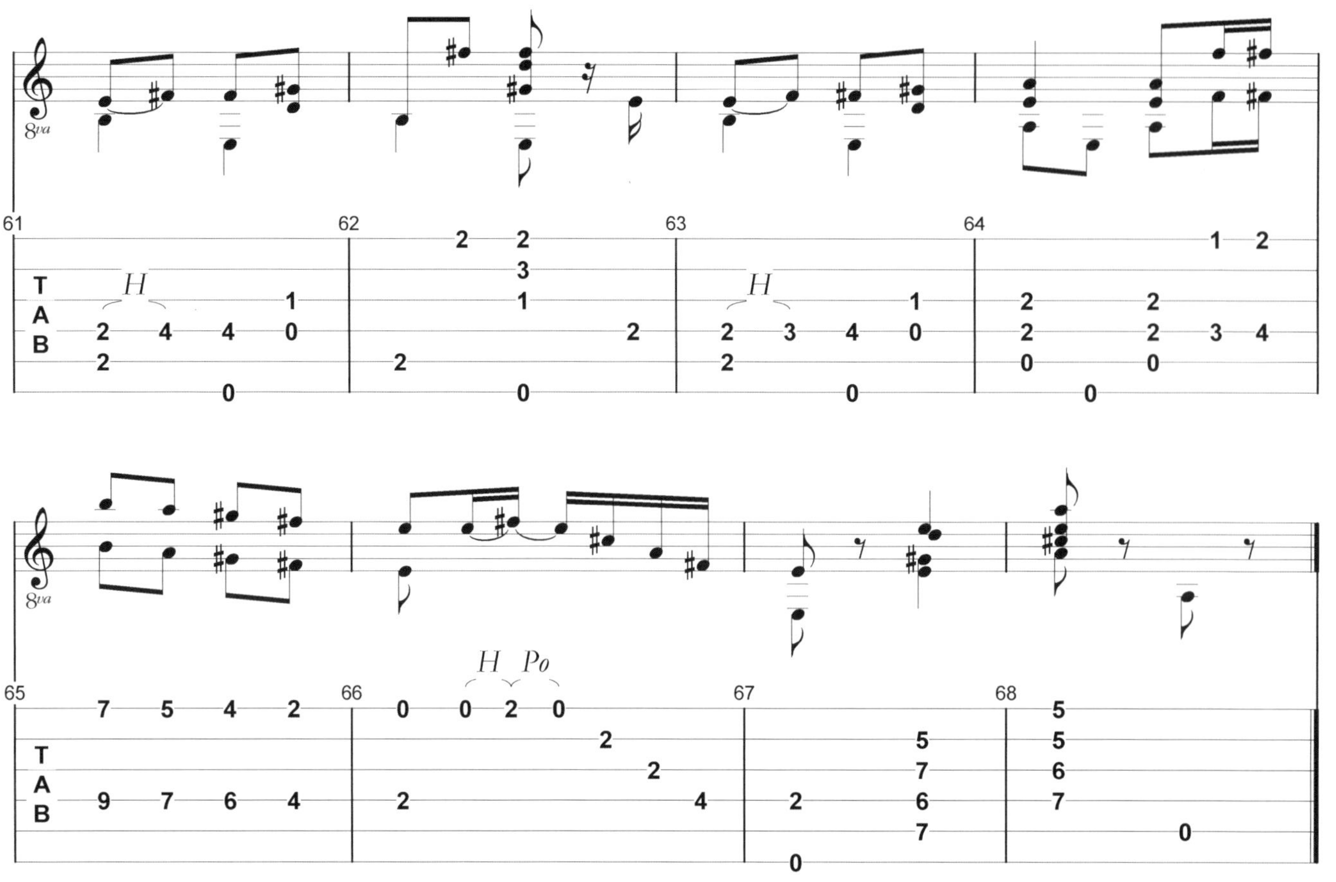
8va
61
62
63
64
65
66
67
68
T
A
B
H
Po

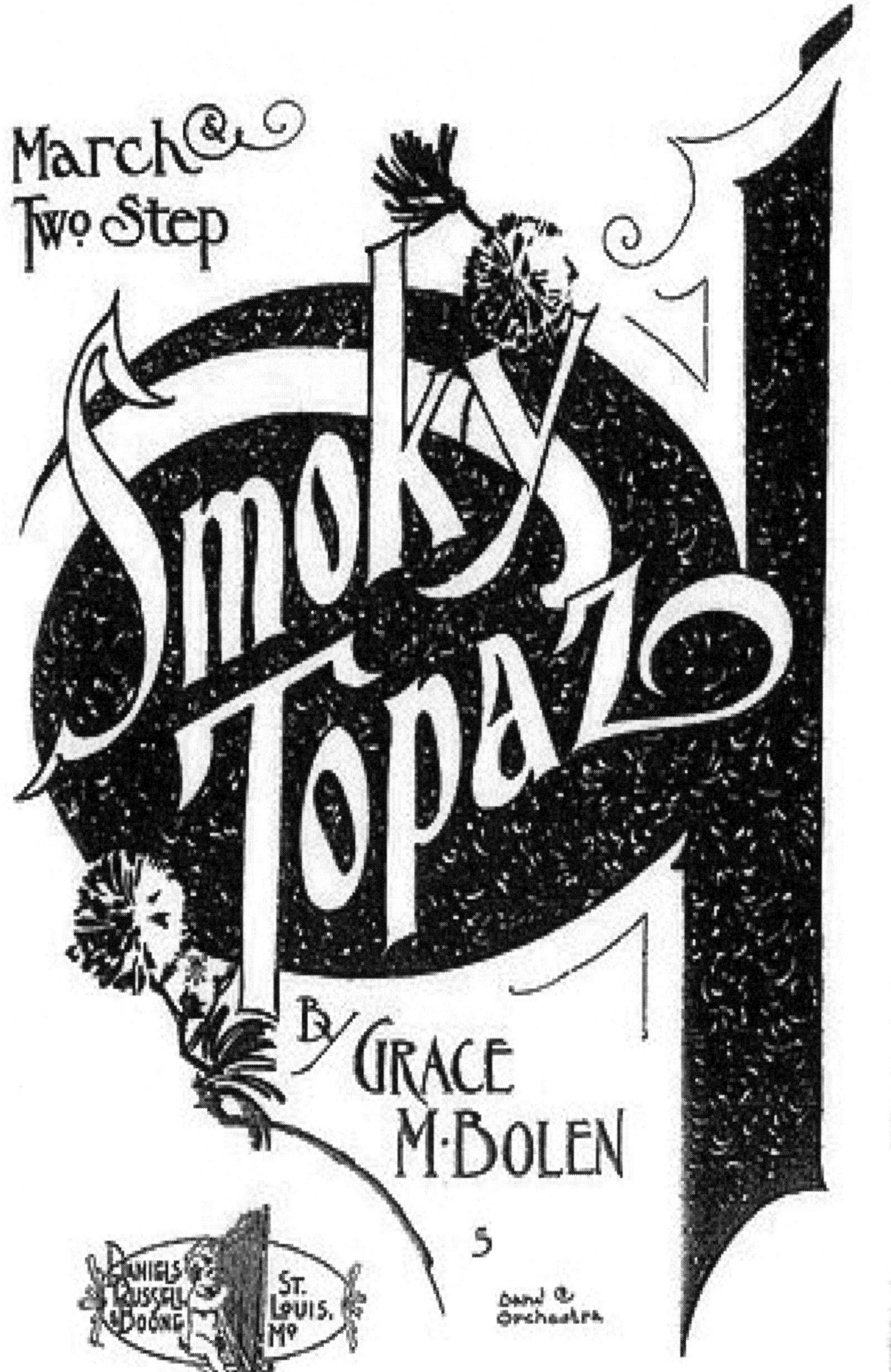
March &
Two Step
Smoky Topaz
By Grace M. Bolen
5
Band & Orchestra
Daniels Russell Boone
St. Louis, Mo

I Love You Truly

Carrie Jacobs-Bond
Arr. Sandy Shalk

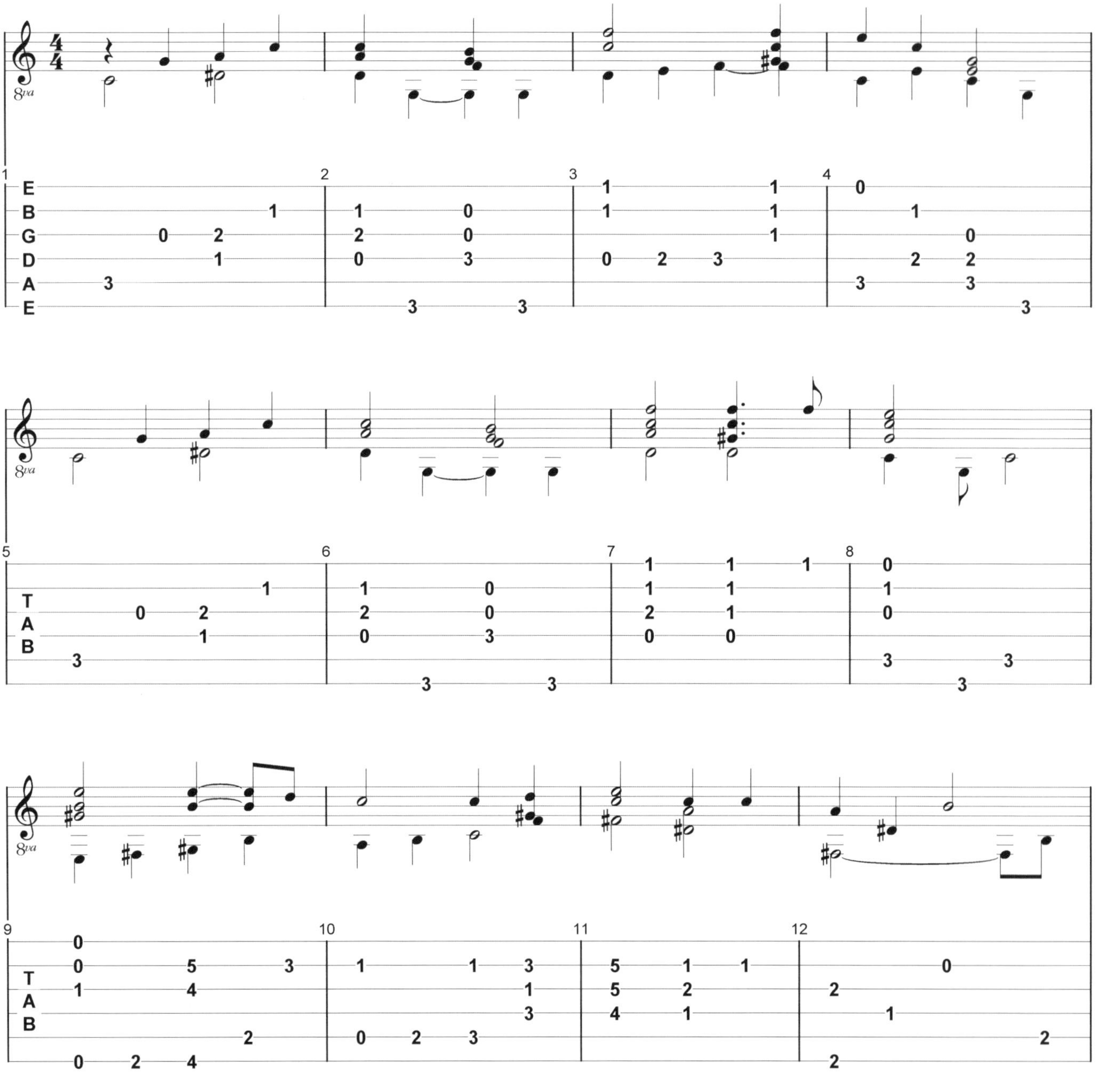

I Love You Truly

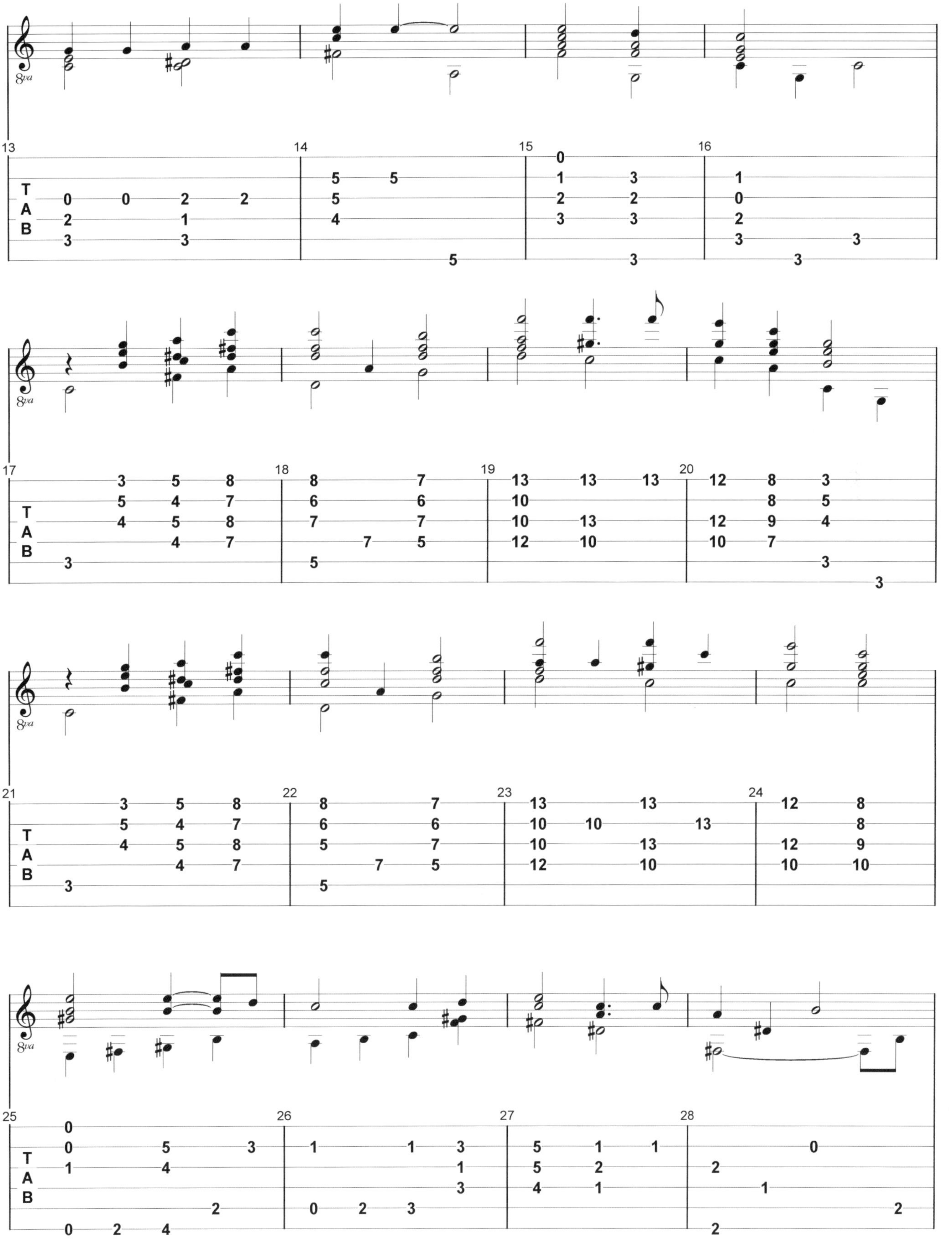

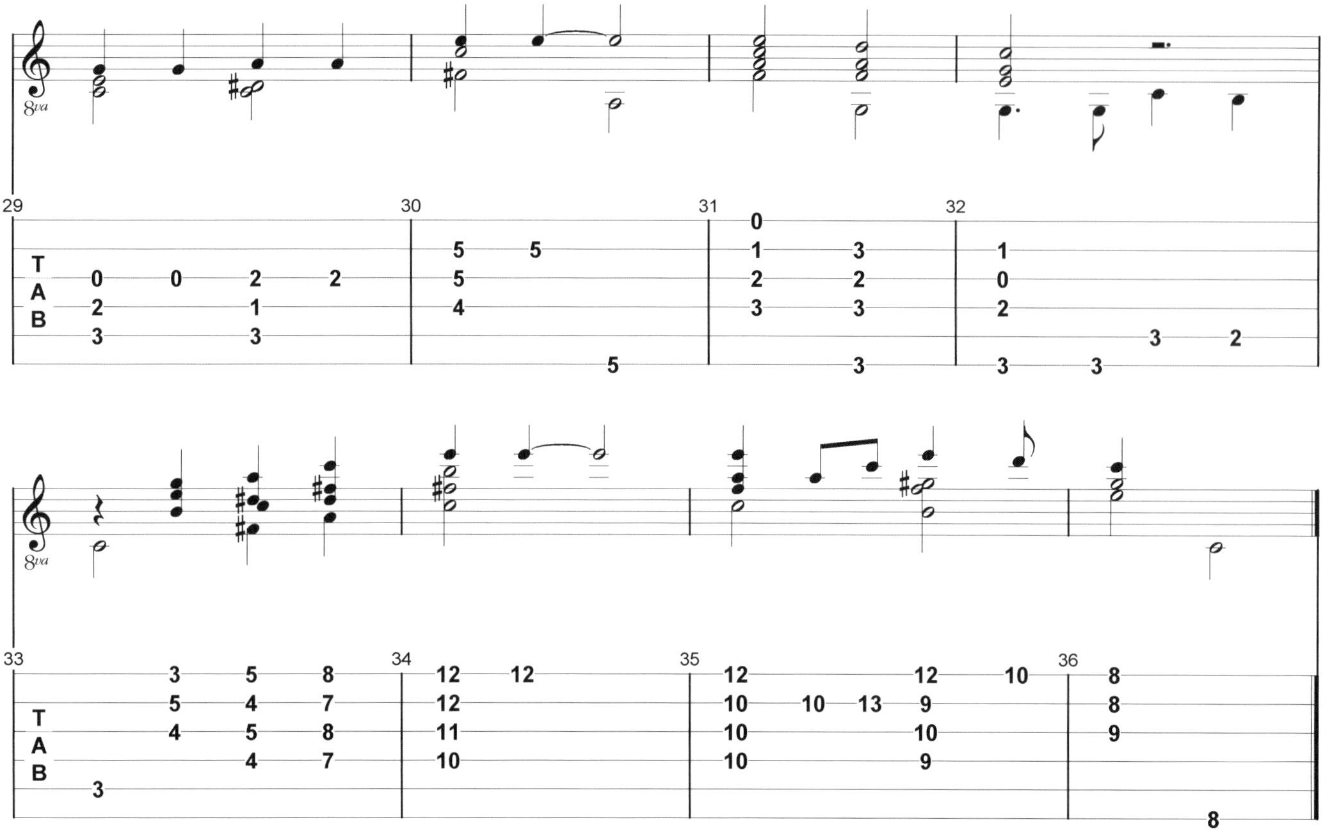
8va
8va

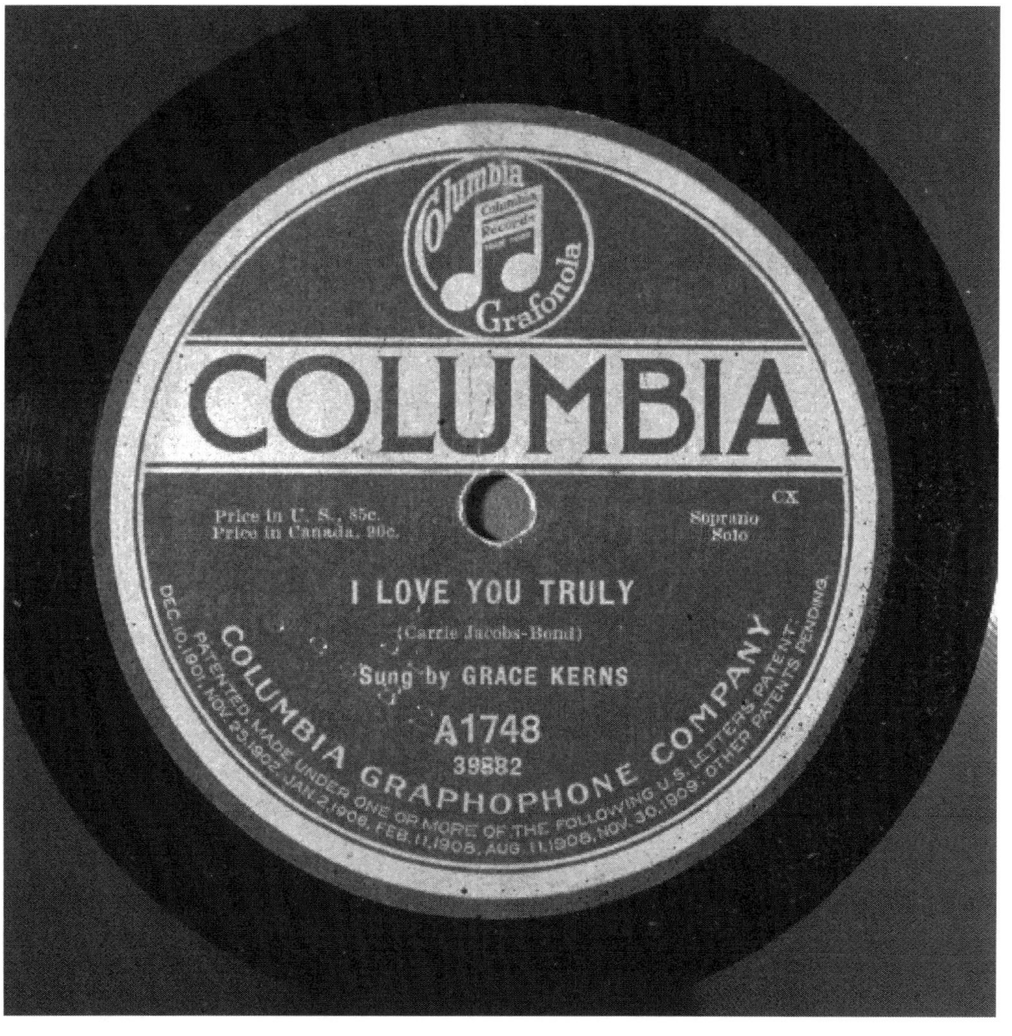
Columbia
Grafonola
COLUMBIA
Price in U. S., 85c.
Price in Canada, 90c.
CX
Soprano
Solo
I LOVE YOU TRULY
(Carrie Jacobs-Bond)
Sung by GRACE KERNS
A1748
39882
COLUMBIA GRAPHOPHONE COMPANY

The Iroquois on Fire

Zella Evans
Arr. Sandy Shalk

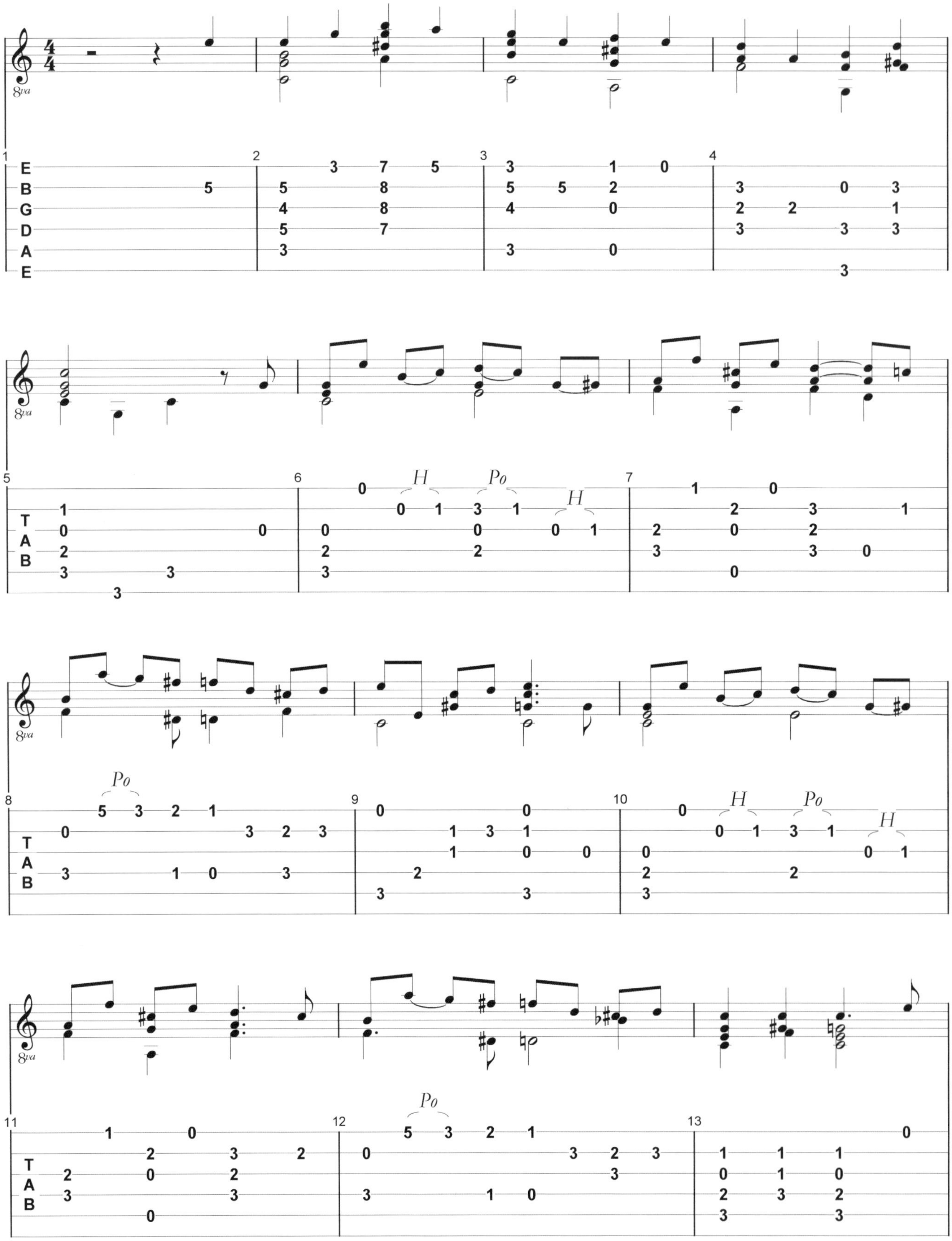

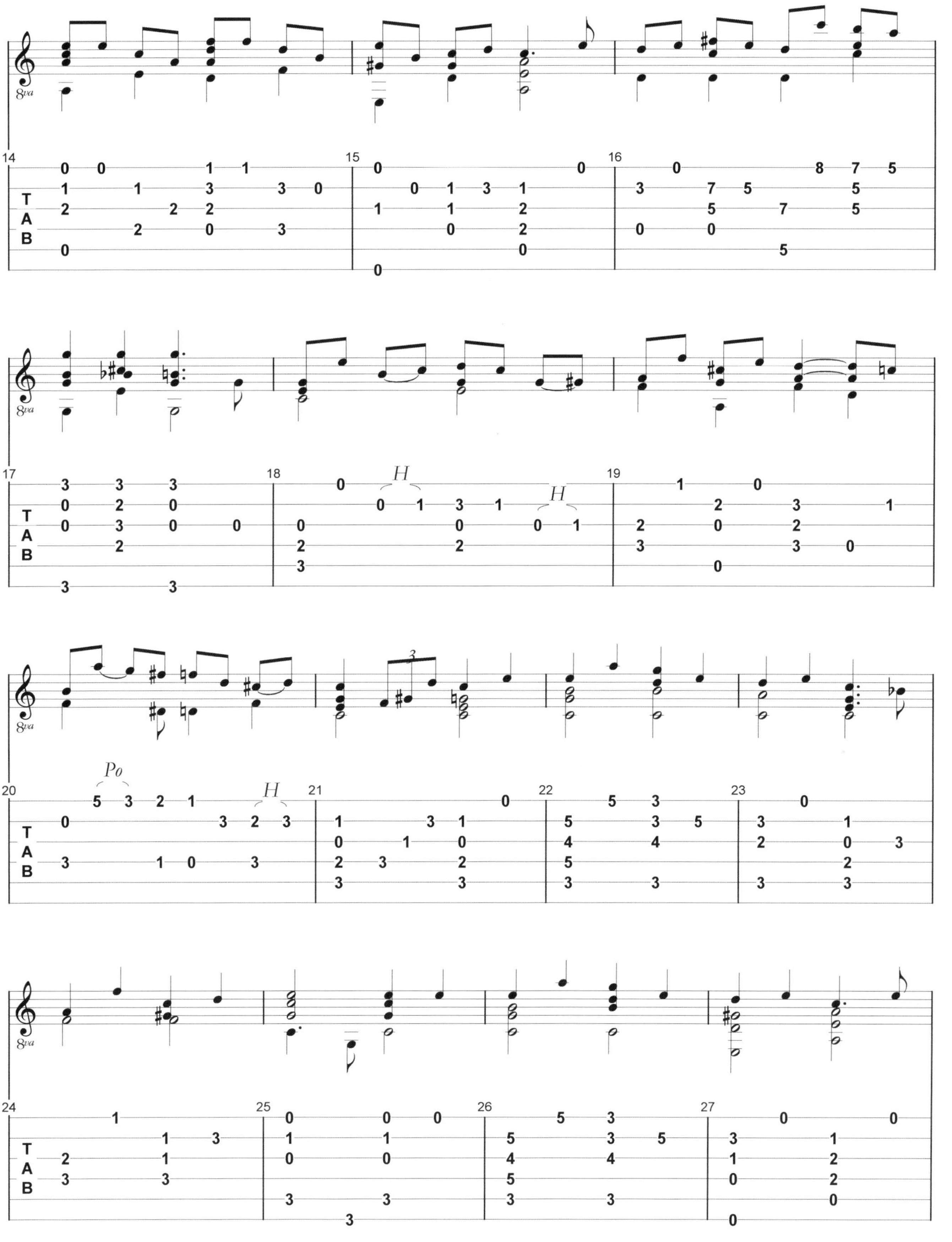
8va
TAB
H
Po

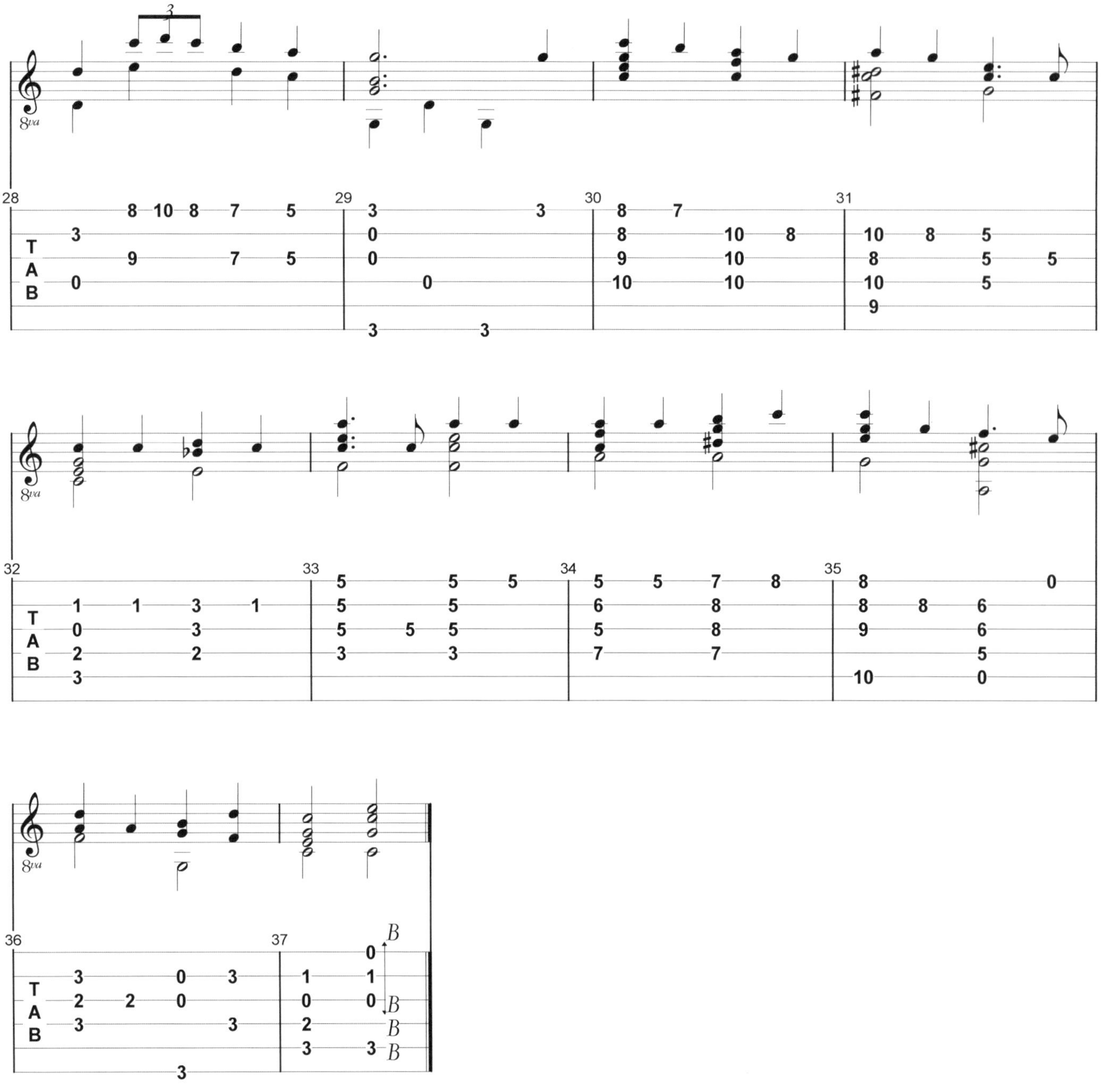
8va
28
29
30
31
TAB
32
33
34
35
36
37
B
B
B
B

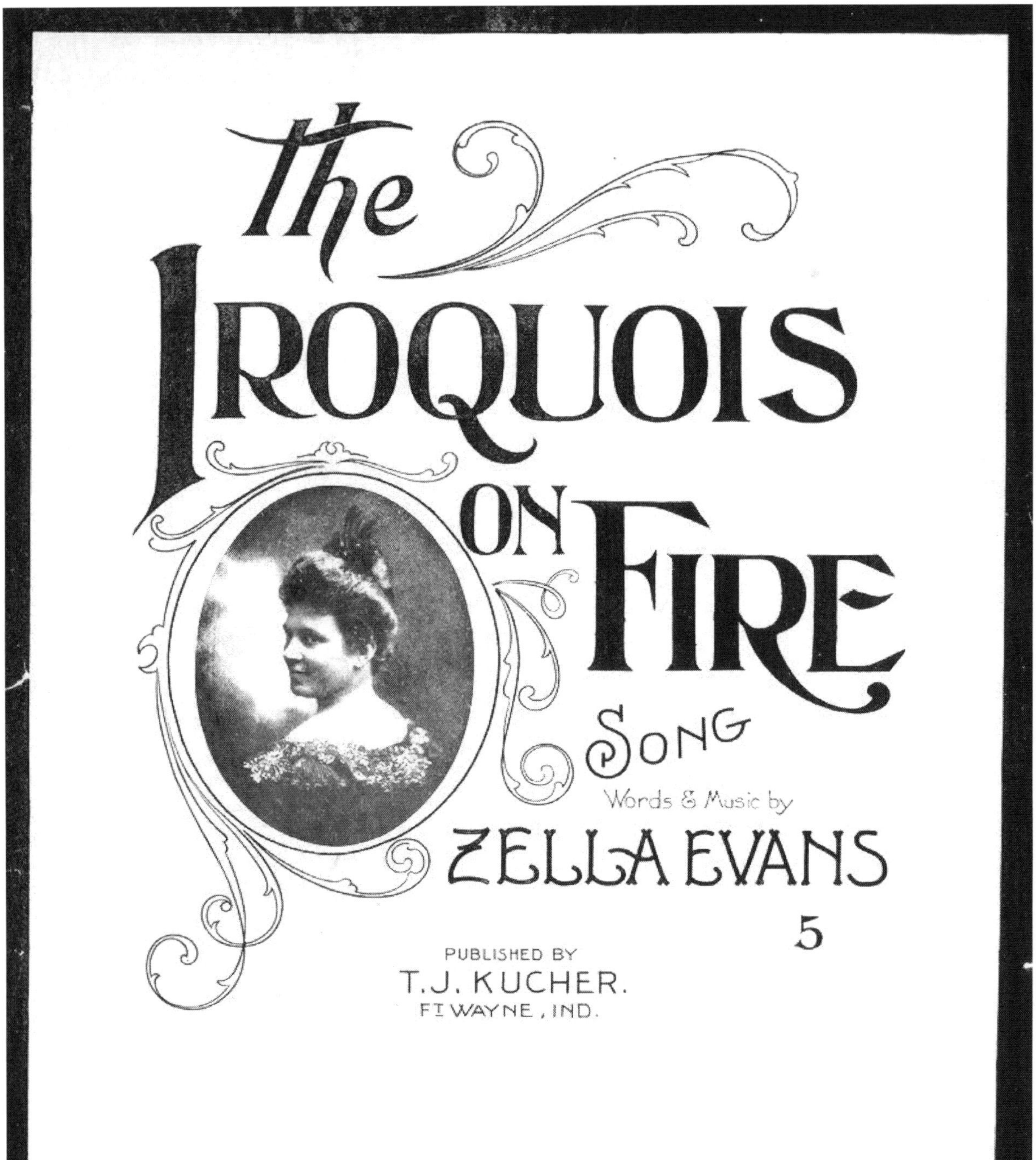

the
IROQUOIS
ON FIRE
SONG
Words & Music by
ZELLA EVANS
5
PUBLISHED BY
T.J. KUCHER.
FT WAYNE, IND.

The End of a Perfect Day

Carrie Jacobs-Bond
Arr. Sandy Shalk

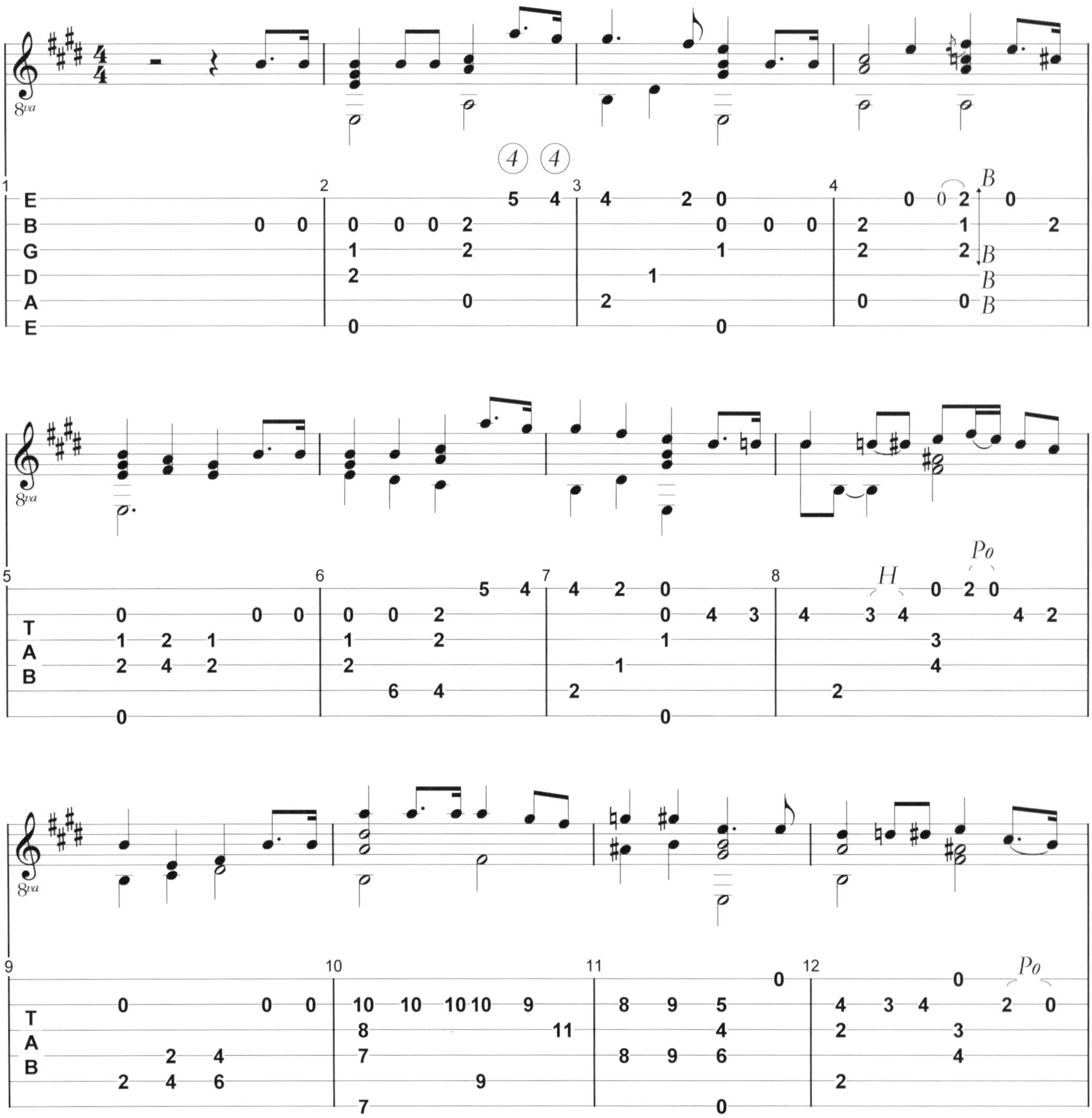

The End of a Perfect Day

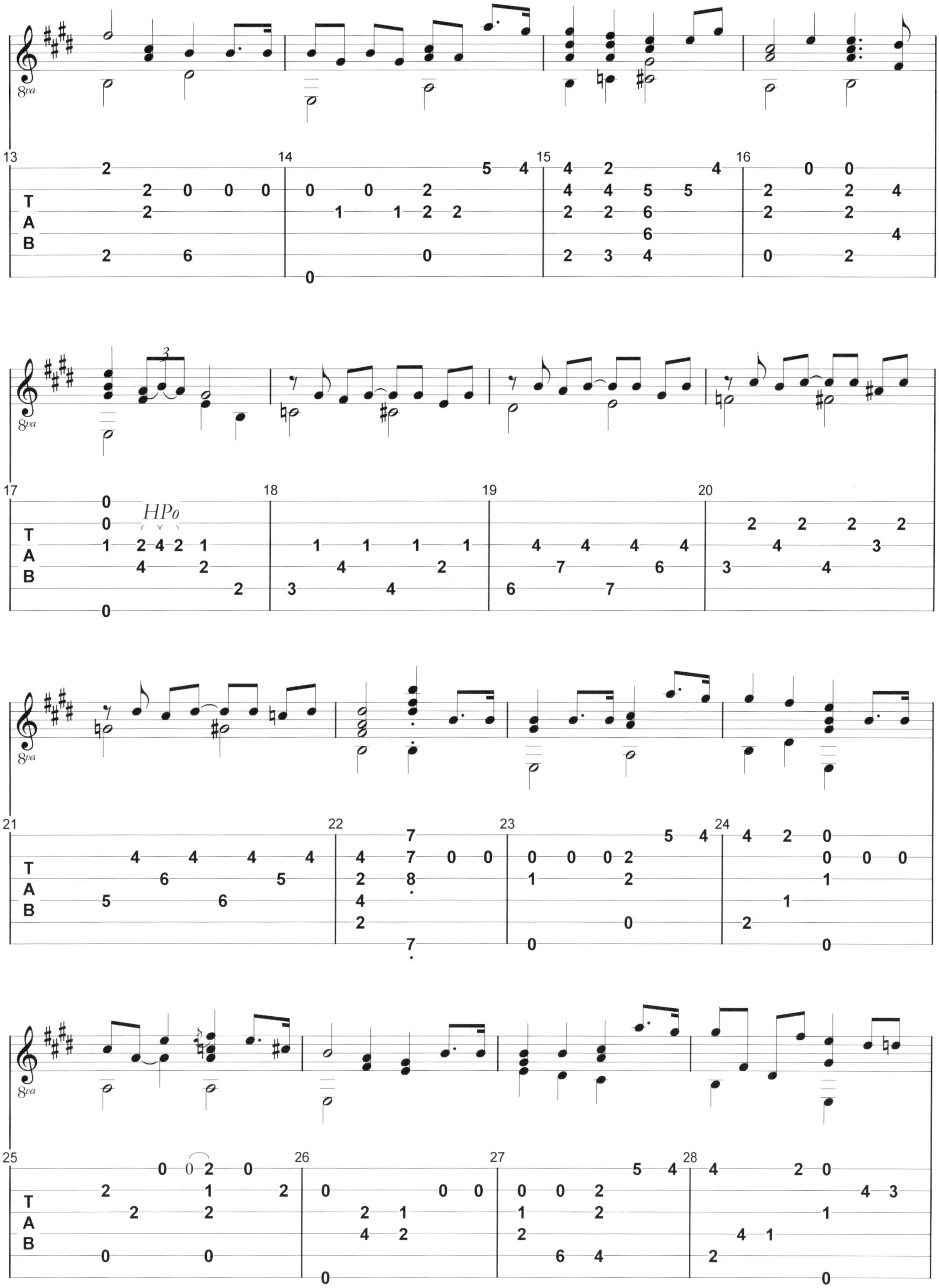

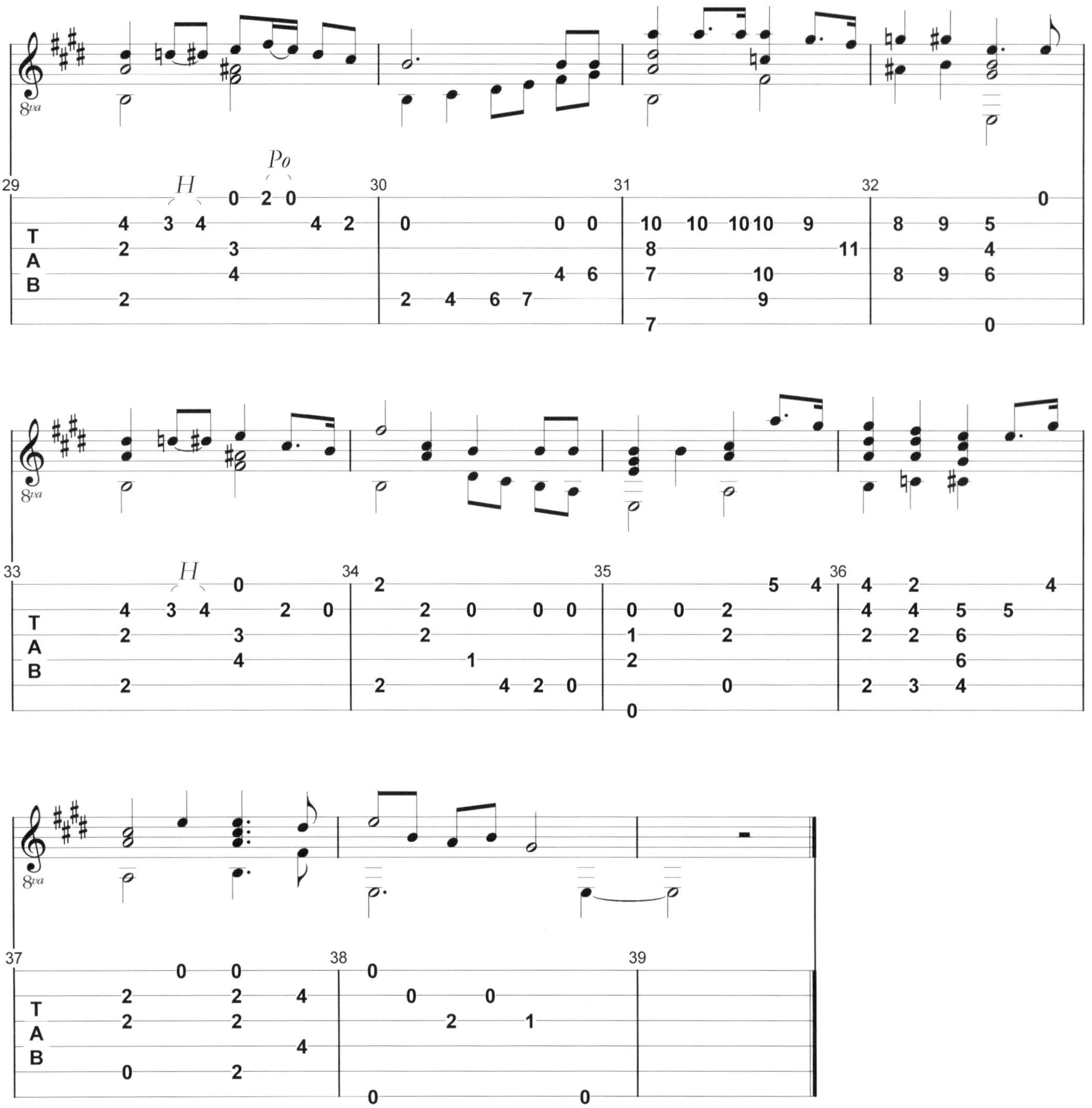
8va
H
Po

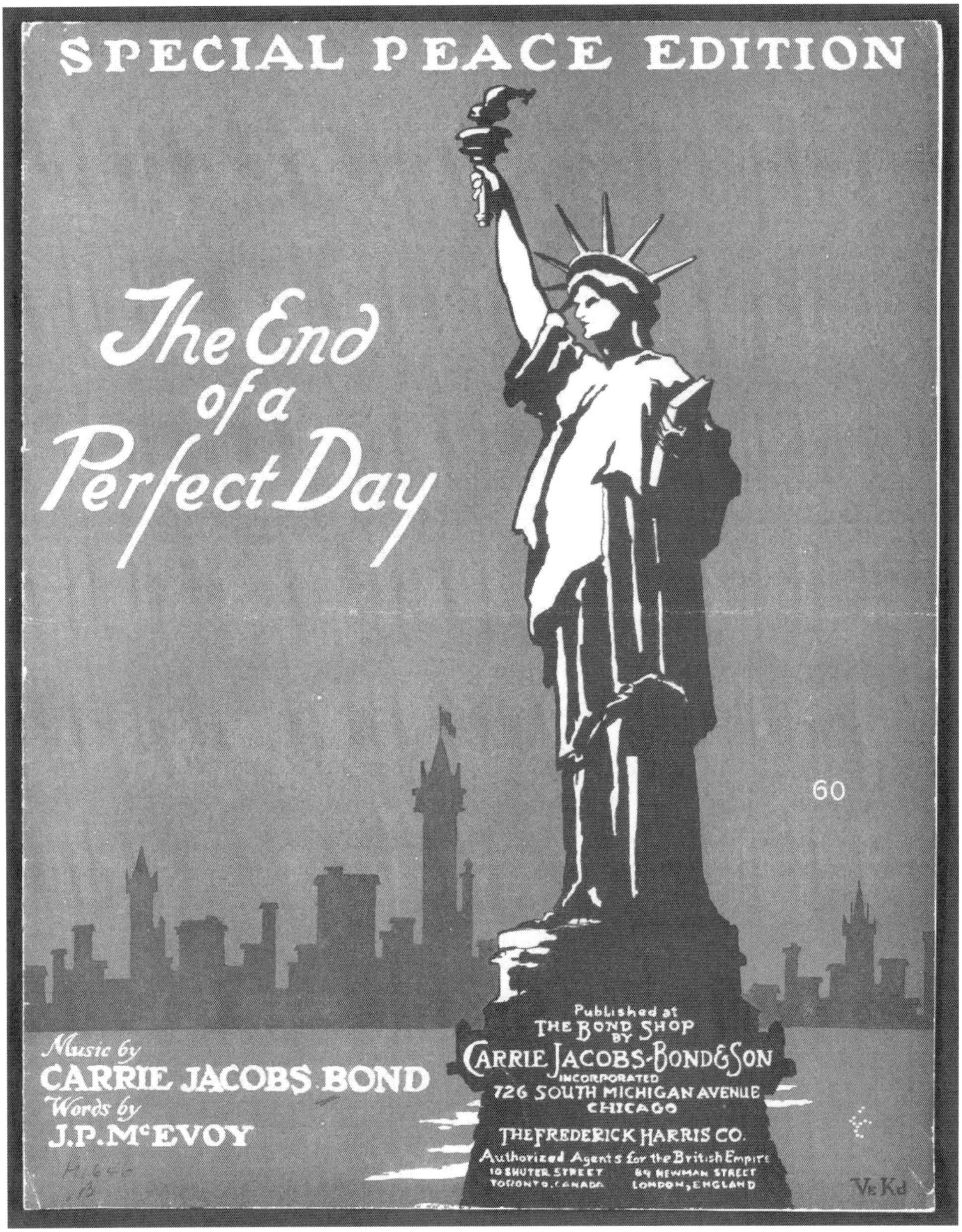
SPECIAL PEACE EDITION
The End of a Perfect Day
60
Music by
CARRIE JACOBS BOND
Words by
J.P. McEVOY
Published at
THE BOND SHOP
BY
CARRIE JACOBS-BOND & SON
INCORPORATED
726 SOUTH MICHIGAN AVENUE
CHICAGO
THE FREDERICK HARRIS CO.
Authorized Agents for the British Empire
10 SHUTER STREET
TORONTO, CANADA
64 NEWMAN STREET
LONDON, ENGLAND

My Rose of Argentine

Norma Gray
Arr. Sandy Shalk

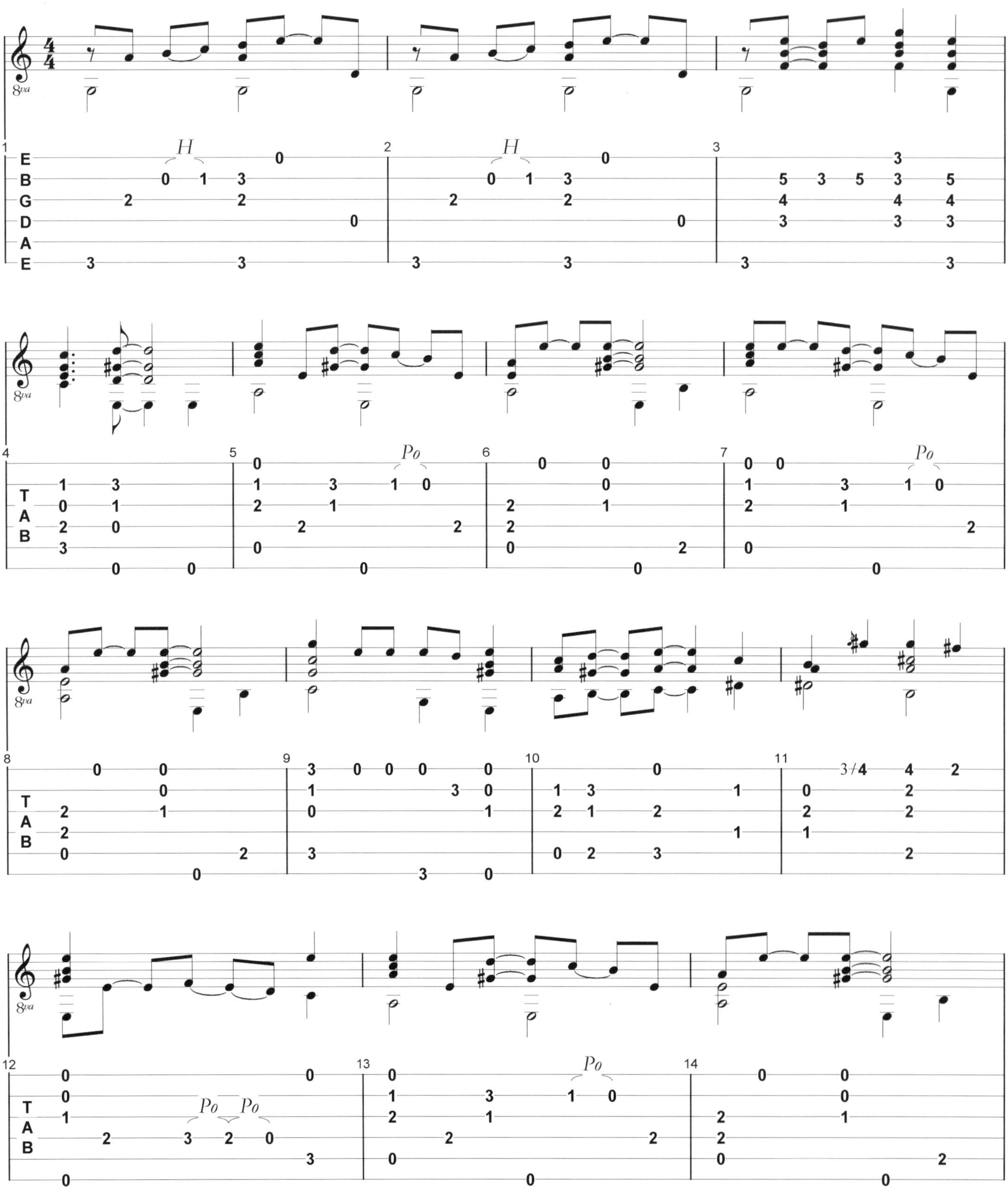

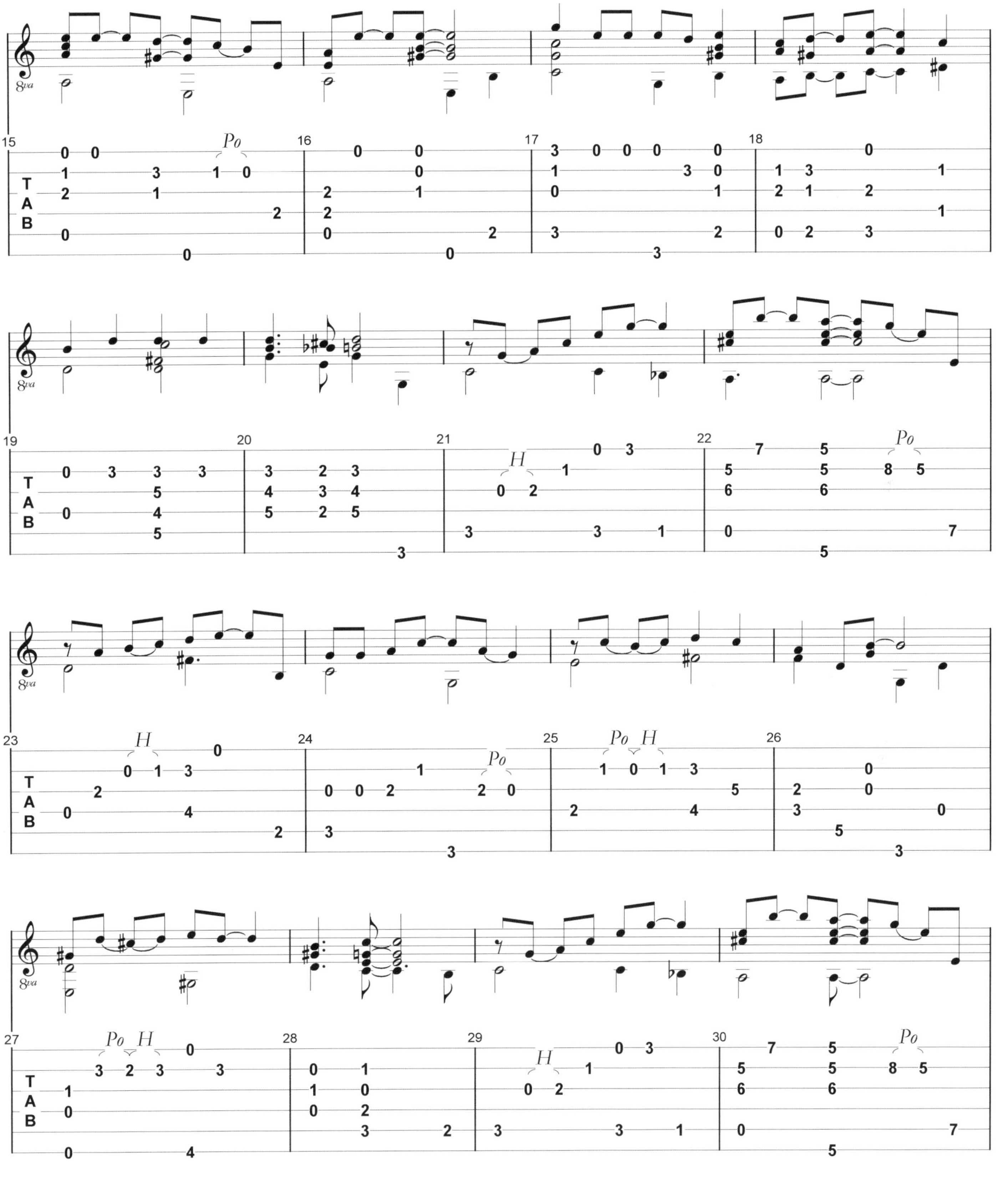
8va
15
16
17
18
19
20
21
22
23
24
25
26
27
28
29
30
TAB
Po
H

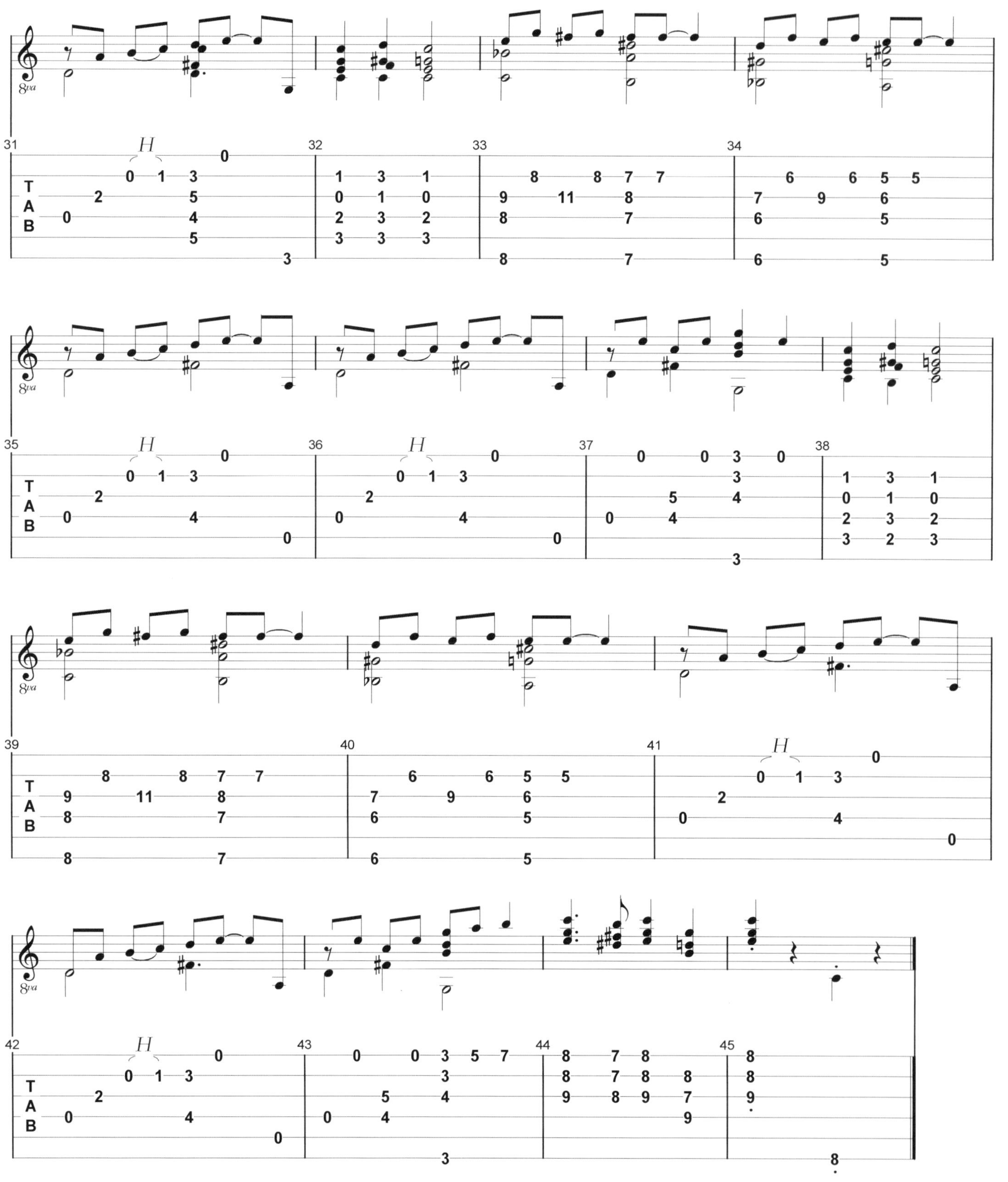

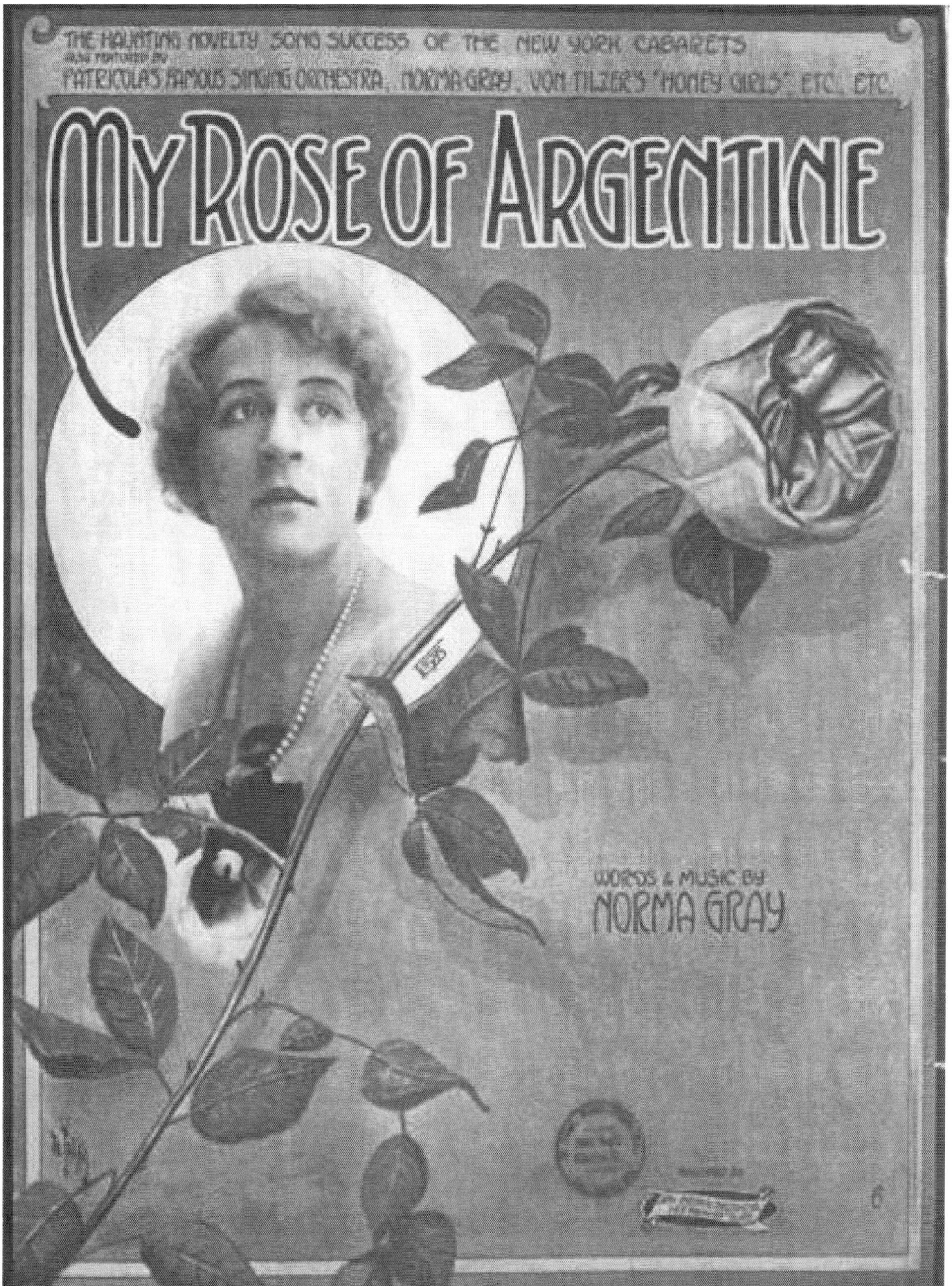
THE HAUNTING NOVELTY SONG SUCCESS OF THE NEW YORK CABARETS
ALSO FEATURED BY
PATRICOLA'S FAMOUS SINGING ORCHESTRA, NORMA GRAY, VON TILZER'S "HONEY GIRLS" ETC., ETC.
MY ROSE OF ARGENTINE
WORDS & MUSIC BY
NORMA GRAY
6

11

Your Country Needs You

Emily Wood Bower
Arr. Sandy Shalk

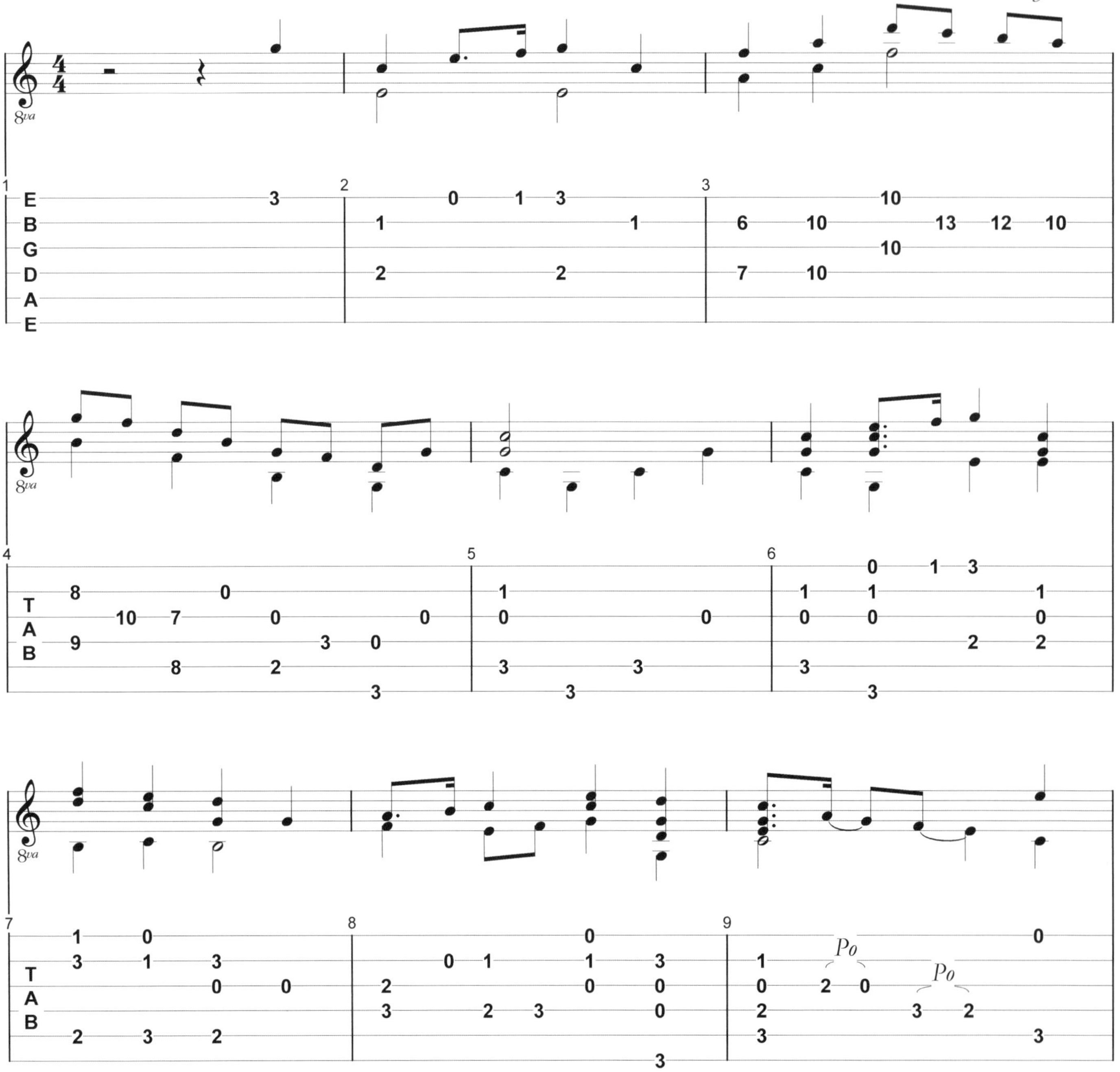

Your Country Needs You

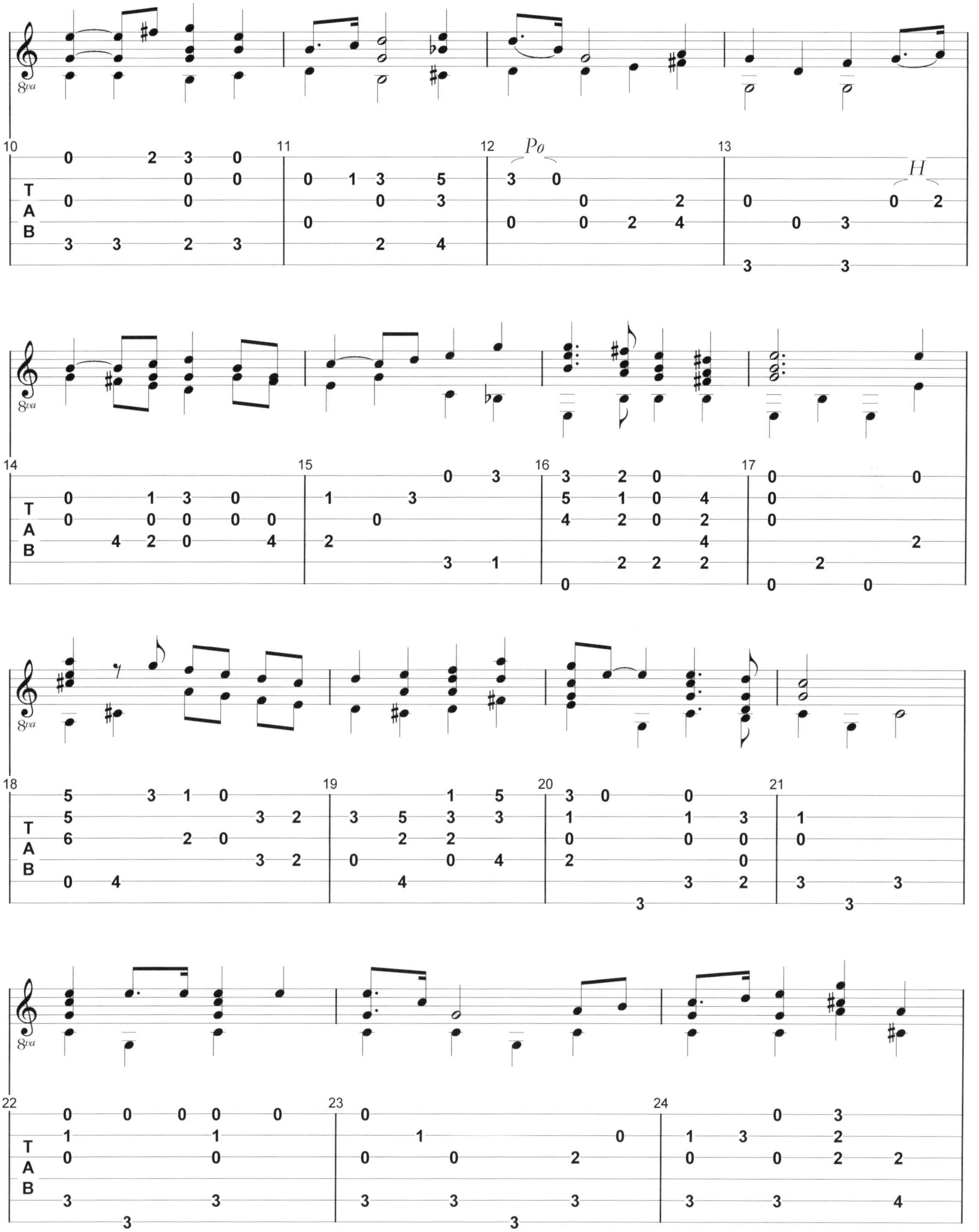

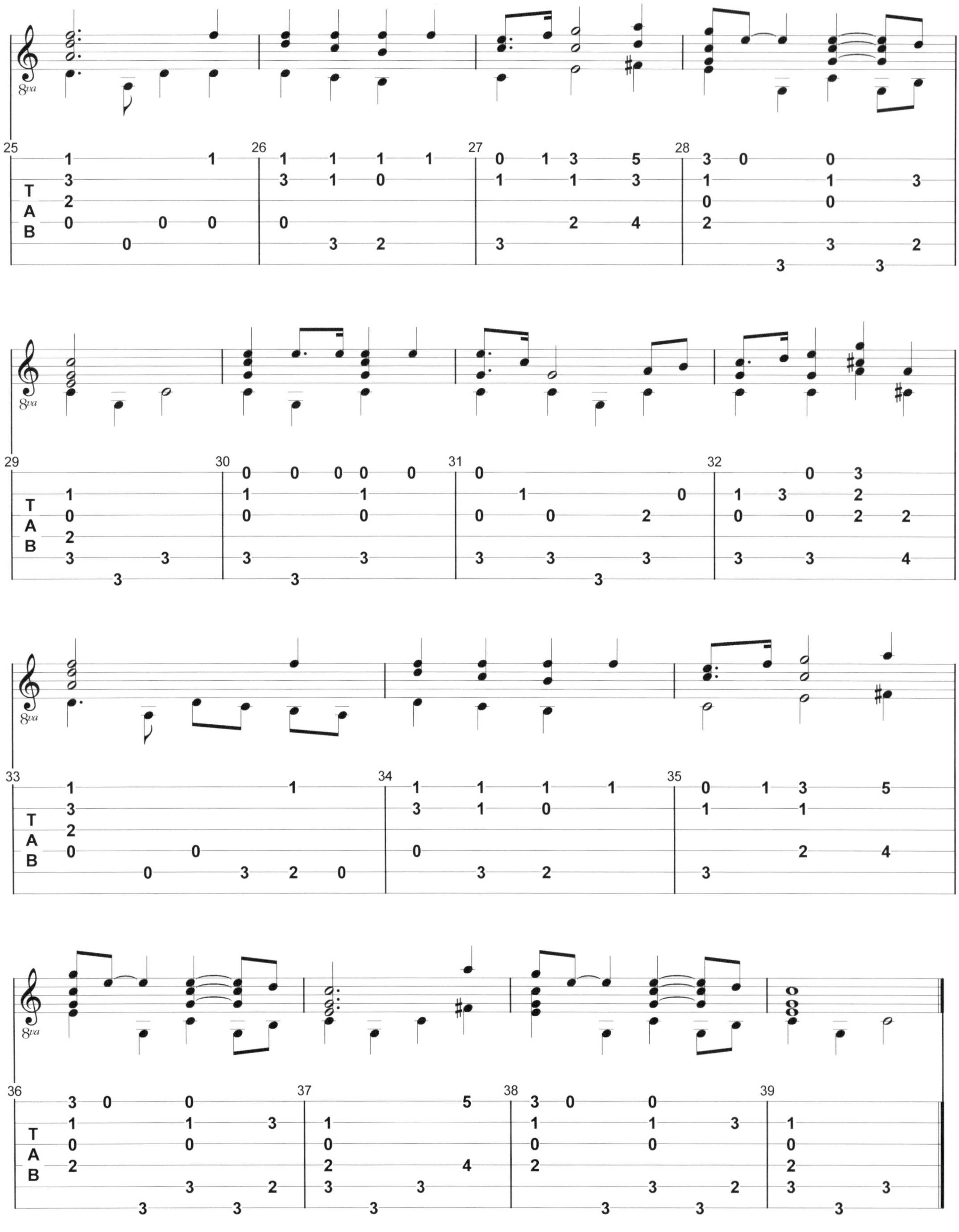
8va
T
A
B

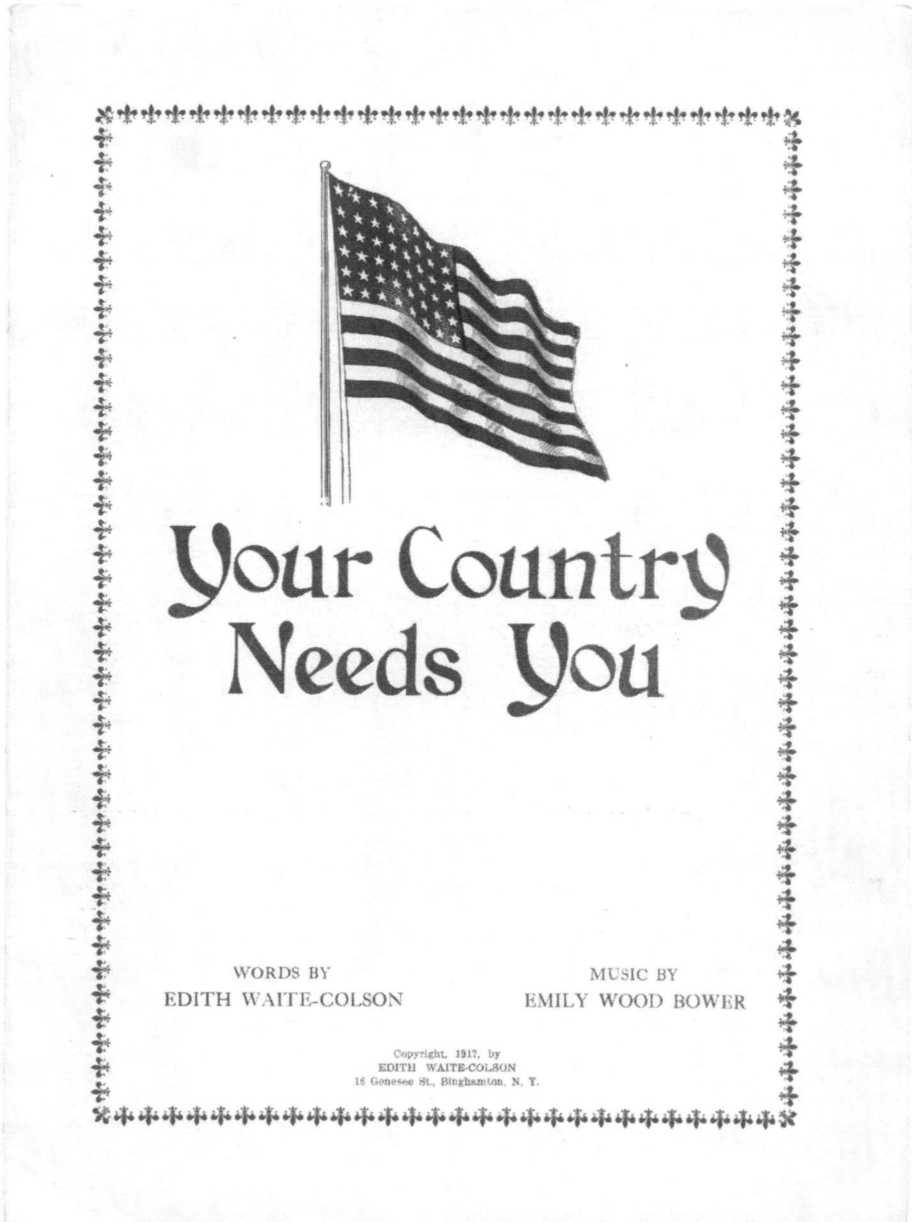
Your Country
Needs You
WORDS BY
EDITH WAITE-COLSON
MUSIC BY
EMILY WOOD BOWER
Copyright, 1917, by
EDITH WAITE-COLSON
16 Genesee St., Binghamton, N. Y.

12

Down Hearted Blues

Lovie Austin
Arr. Sandy Shalk

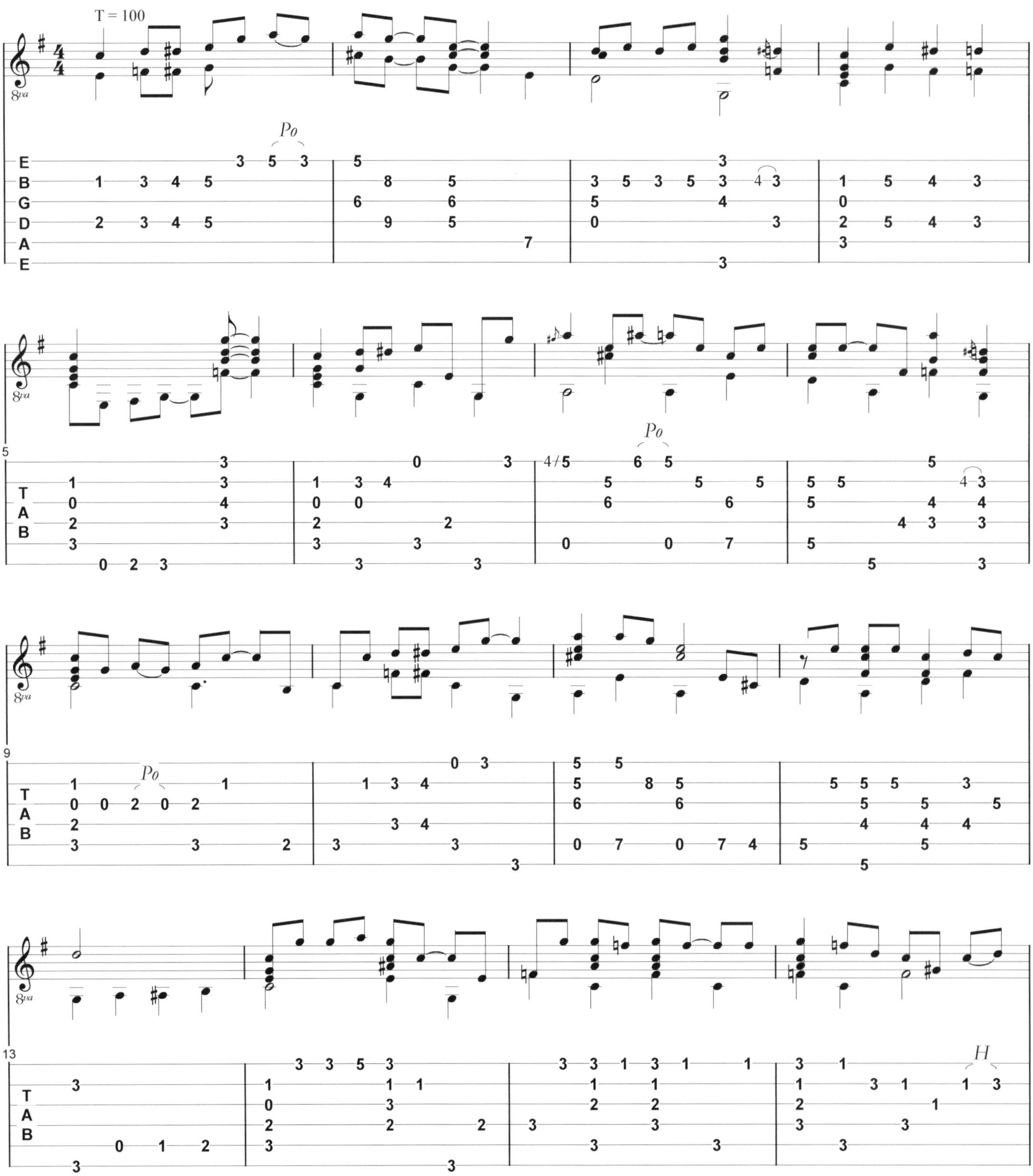

Down Hearted Blues

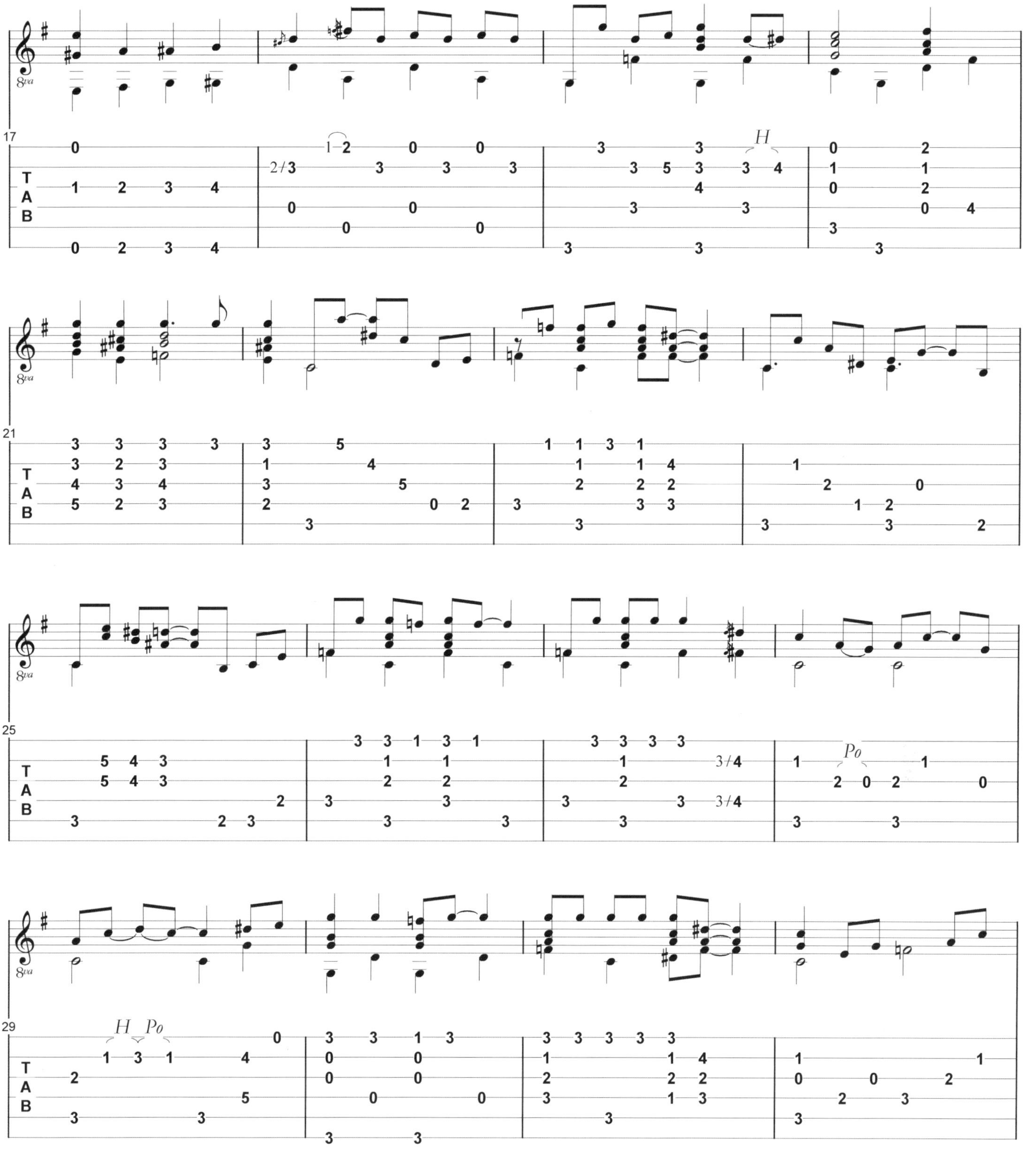

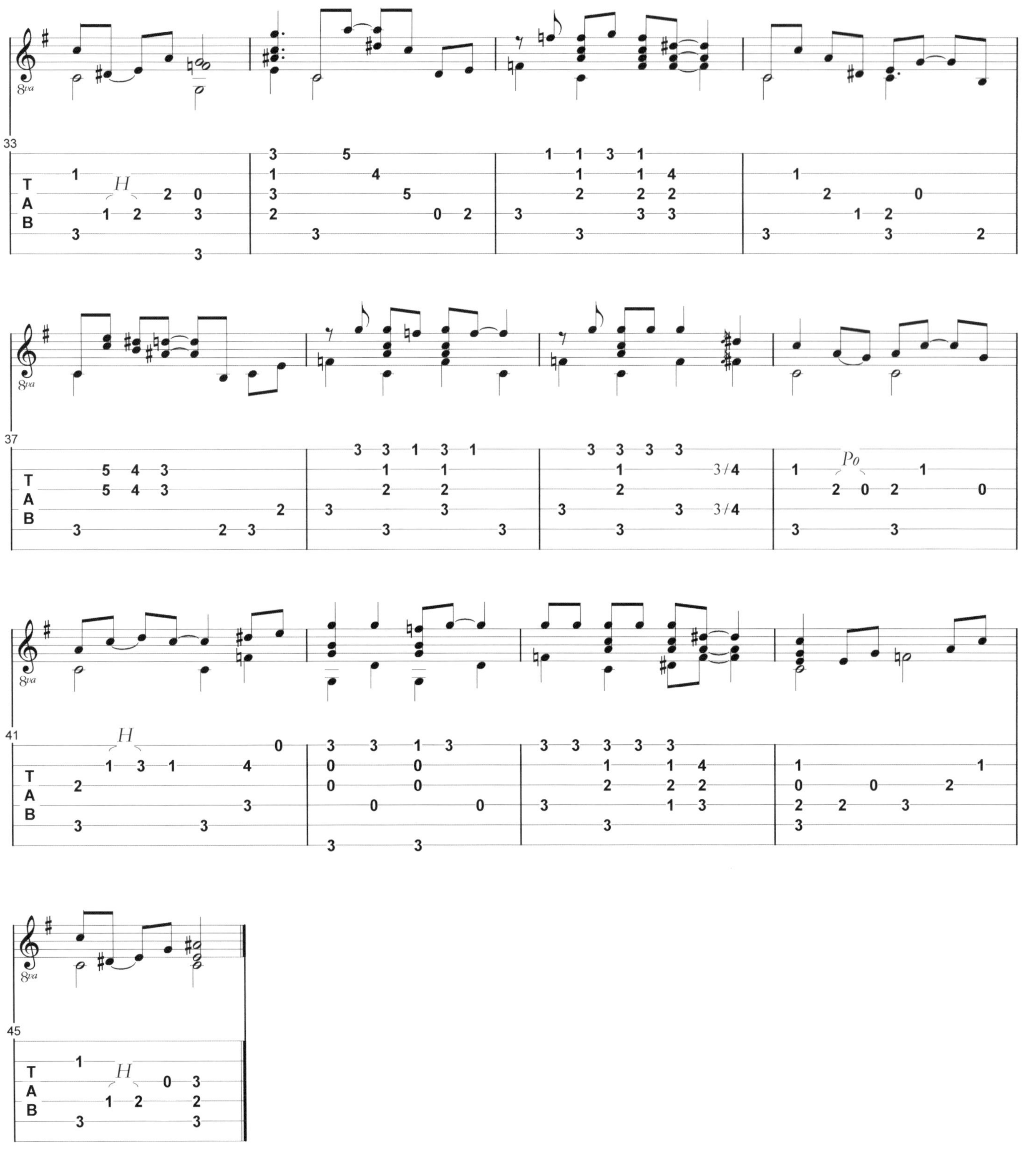
8va
T
A
B
H
Po

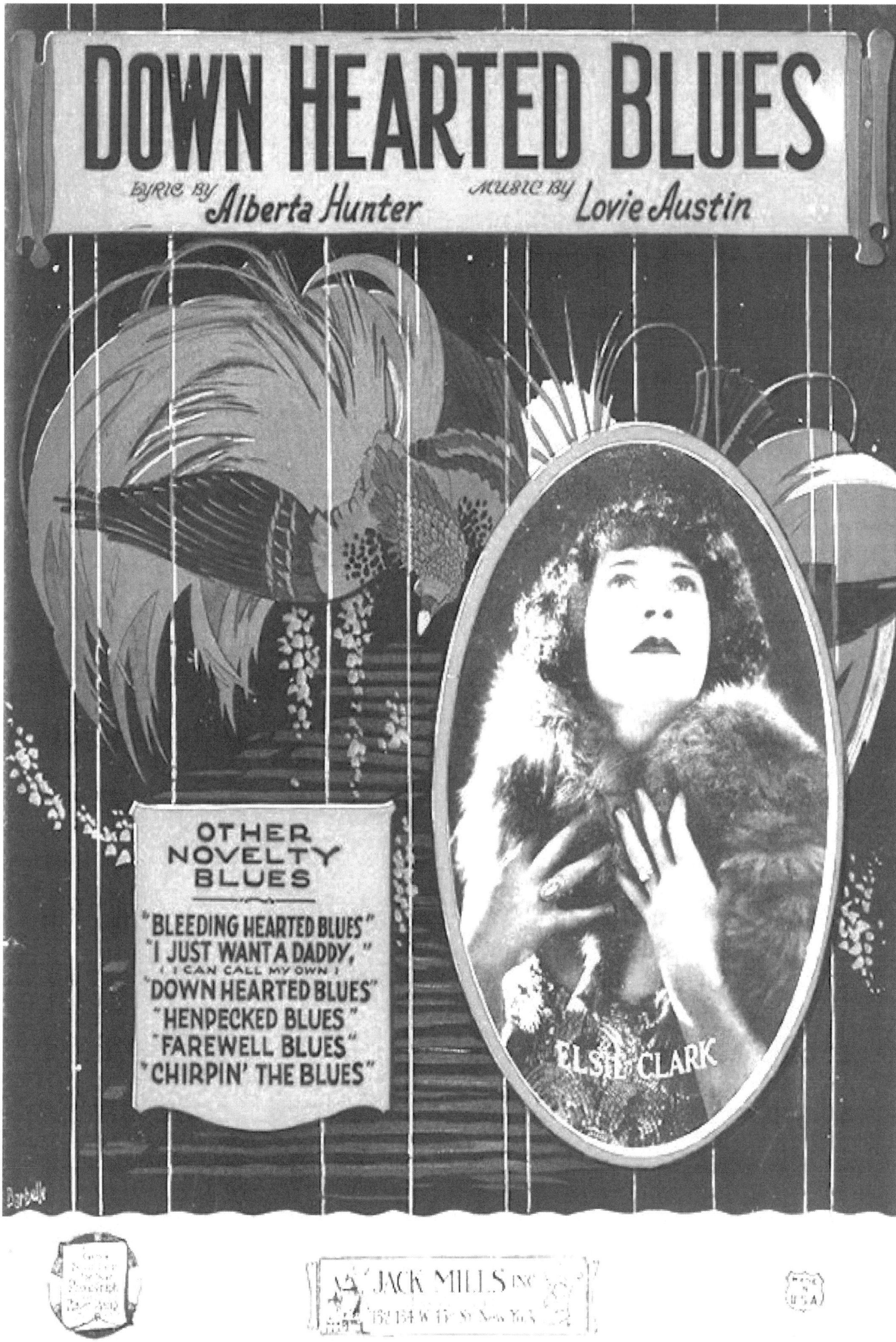
DOWN HEARTED BLUES
LYRIC BY Alberta Hunter
MUSIC BY Lovie Austin
OTHER NOVELTY BLUES
"BLEEDING HEARTED BLUES"
"I JUST WANT A DADDY," (I CAN CALL MY OWN)
"DOWN HEARTED BLUES"
"HENPECKED BLUES"
"FAREWELL BLUES"
"CHIRPIN' THE BLUES"
ELSIE CLARK
JACK MILLS INC
New York

Other Mel Bay Fingerstyle Guitar Solo Books

Art of Gospel Guitar/Dropped-D Tuning (McMeen)
Celtic Guitar Delights (McMeen)
Celtic Guitar Treasures (McMeen)
DADGAD and DCDGCD Tunings (Henigan)
DADGAD Blues (MacKillop)
DADGAD Easy Christmas Favorites (MacKillop)
DADGAD Encyclopedia (Goodin)
DADGAD Gospel (McMeen/Shalk)
DADGAD & Dropped-D Photo Chords (W. Bay)
DADGAD & Dropped-D Photo Chords - Left Handed Edition (W. Bay)
DADGAD Ragtime and Early Jazz (MacKillop)
Dropped-D Guitar: Bach to Blues (Marshall)
Easy DADGAD Celtic Guitar Book (MacKillop)
Easy DADGAD Classics for Acoustic Guitar (MacKillop)
El McMeen: Solo Guitar Serenade
Fiddle Tunes in DADGAD (Young)
Frailing the Guitar (Baughman)
Islands: Guitar Interpretations of Celtic Music (Hinchliffe)
Martin Simpson: Just a Closer Walk with Thee/Assorted Open Tunings
Midsummer Moon (Petteway)
New Directions in Open G Guitar Tuning (McMeen/Shalk)
Scottish 18th-Century Guitar Tunes/Open D Tuning (MacKillop)
Steve Baughman's Celtic Guitar Method
Strike Up the Band (McMeen)
The Art of Dropped-D Guitar (McMeen)
The Glory of CGDGAD Guitar Tuning (McMeen/Shalk)
Understanding DADGAD (Young)
Whispering Stones (Petteway)
101 Easy Fingerstyle Guitar Solos (McCabe)
All-Time Favorite Parking Lot Fingersyle Guitar Solos (McAdoo)
American Fiddle Tunes for Acoustic Guitar (Matteson)
American Treasures (Lester/Piburn)
An American Christmas (M. Lord)
Ashokan Farewell Fingerstyle Guitar Solo (Jay Ungar/Lehmann-Haupt)
Ballads and Songs of the Civil War for Guitar (Silverman)
British Fingerpicking Guitar (Grossman)
Christmas Encyclopedia: Fingerstyle Edition (Eckels)
Christmas Songs for Fingerstyle Guitar (Flint)
Easiest Fingerpicking Guitar Solos (W. Bay/Flint)
Easiest Fingerpicking Guitar for Children (McCabe)
Fingerpicking Guitar Tune Book (Flint)
Fingerstyle Guitar Tunes-Beautiful American Airs and Ballads (Gonzalez)
Fingerstyle Guitar Tunes-Beautiful Airs and Ballads of the British Isles (Gonzalez)
Fingerstyle Guitar Tunes-Christmas in the British Isles (Gonzalez)
Folk songs and Dances of the Jewish People for Acoustic Guitar (Back)
Folk Songs from the Appalachian Mountains for Acoustic Guitar (Matteson)
Global Adventures for Fingerstyle Guitarists (Eckels)
Guitar Music of Cuba (Barreiro)

WWW.MELBAY.COM